Thuggery: How European powers divided and shaped the Arab World

Europeans divided & shaped Arab World

DM Ole Kiminta

Published by KBros, 2025.

While every precaution has been taken in the preparation of this book, the publisher assumes no responsibility for errors or omissions, or for damages resulting from the use of the information contained herein.

EUROPEANS DIVIDED & SHAPED ARAB WORLD

First edition. May 10, 2025.

Copyright © 2025 DM Ole Kiminta.

ISBN: 978-1069498601

Written by DM Ole Kiminta.

Also by DM Ole Kiminta

How the Western Democracies failed the world
Supporting Refugees in their Homelands
Dissuading Global War Mongers:
Dissuading war mongers
La Libération Monétaire en Afrique
Canada Post: Management failure to modernise mail systems
Canada Post management failure to modernise mail systems
Canada Post: Management failure to modernise mail systems
Live to be 200
Aim to live for 200
Aim to live to be 200
Western democracies failed the world economies
Wrong foot forward: US-Canada trade wars
Canada begs to differ: Never a 51st state of USA
Tethered to the Kitchen
Nous ne pouvons pas être le 51e État des États-Unis
Nous ne serons jamais le 51ème état des États-Unis.
The Nephilim and the erosion of moral boundaries
Every human is an advocate for World Peace
The diplomatic dilemma of Western Sahara
Every human: Advocate for World Peace
The last blue planet
Europeans divided & shaped Arab World

Table of Contents

Chapter 1: The historical context of Arab identity 1
Chapter 2: European Interests in the Arab World 6
Chapter 3: The Sykes-Picot Agreement 11
Chapter 4: Consequences of the Sykes-Picot agreement 16
Chapter 5: The role of foreign intervention in modern conflicts 20
Chapter 6: Reassessing borders and identities 28
Chapter 7: Conclusion: lessons from history 33
Chapter 8: Introduction to Palestinian land rights 38
Chapter 9: Thuggery: Destruction of Palestinian land 43
Chapter 10: Historical analysis of land displacement in Palestine 48
Chapter 11: Case studies of specific Palestinian communities affected by thuggery 53
Chapter 12: International law and land rights in Palestine 57
Chapter 13: The role of non-Governmental organisations in advocating for Palestinian land 62
Chapter 14: Media representation of land destruction in Palestinian areas 67
Chapter 15: Community resilience: Palestinian responses to land loss 72
Chapter 16: Economic consequences of land destruction on Palestinian livelihoods 77
Chapter 17: Cultural heritage and land loss in Palestinian history 80
Chapter 18: Conclusion: Pathways to justice for Palestinian land rights . 85
Chapter 19: The price of peace: Analysing the aftermath of the October 7th attack 90
Chapter 20: The Israeli response 98
Chapter 21: The humanitarian crisis 103
Chapter 22: Global reactions and responses 107
Chapter 23: Media coverage and narrative 112
Chapter 24: Long-term consequences 117
Chapter 25: Lessons learned and moving forward 122
Recommended reading & references: 126

For those who have perished because of human foolishness and greed
(R.I.P.)

To the reader:

Because of the sensitivity and nature of existing perpetual conflicts between Arabs and Jewish neighbours in the Middle East, I had to constantly keep reminding myself of two very precious things necessary for those who write books or newspapers: I had to be IMPERTIAL and non-judgemental.

Derek Ole Kiminta

How European powers divided and shaped the Arab World

Chapter 1: The historical context of Arab identity

The rise of Arab nationalism
The rise of Arab nationalism in the early 20th century was largely a response to the colonial ambitions of European powers, which sought to carve up the Middle East for their own geopolitical interests. As the Ottoman Empire began to weaken, Arab intellectuals and leaders started to advocate for a sense of unity among Arab peoples. They emphasised a shared language, culture, and history, which became the foundation for a national identity that transcended local loyalties. This burgeoning nationalism was fuelled by a desire for self-determination and resistance against foreign domination, particularly in the wake of the disintegration of Ottoman control.

The Sykes-Picot Agreement of 1916 was a pivotal moment in the history of Arab nationalism. In this secret arrangement, Britain and France divided the Middle Eastern territories of the collapsing Ottoman Empire into spheres of influence, with little regard for the ethnic and religious complexities of the region. This betrayal of Arab aspirations for independence, which had been promised in exchange for support against the Ottomans, ignited widespread resentment. The arbitrary borders drawn by European powers disregarded historical tribal boundaries and cultural connections, leading to a fragmented political landscape that would have lasting consequences for the future of the Arab world.

In the aftermath of World War I, the establishment of mandates in the region further entrenched foreign control and deepened the sense of betrayal among Arab populations. The League of Nations sanctioned the British and French mandates, presenting them as a means of preparing territories for self-governance. However, the reality was that European powers maintained significant control over the political and economic affairs of these regions, stifling the aspirations of Arab nationalists. The growing discontent culminated in various uprisings and movements across the region, as leaders sought to rally the Arab population against foreign rule and assert their right to self-determination.

The impact of foreign intervention in Arab conflicts has continued to resonate throughout the 20th and into the 21st century. The artificial borders established post-WWI have contributed to ongoing tensions and conflicts, as ethnic and sectarian divisions were exacerbated by the lack of cohesion among newly formed states. The Cold War further complicated matters, as superpowers intervened in regional disputes, often supporting authoritarian regimes that suppressed nationalist movements. This cycle of foreign interference has perpetuated instability, leading to civil wars and humanitarian crises that continue to plague the Arab world today.

The rise of Arab nationalism, therefore, must be understood in the context of external influences and the historical grievances borne from colonial policies. As Arab peoples sought to assert their identity and claim their rights, they found themselves navigating a landscape fraught with the legacies of betrayal. The struggle for unity and self-determination remains a central theme in the narratives of contemporary Arab nations, highlighting the profound effects of historical events like the Sykes-Picot Agreement and the enduring consequences of foreign intervention. The paths forged by early nationalists continue to influence the aspirations and conflicts of the Arab world, underscoring the complex interplay between identity, history, and power.

Book Overview:

WHEN WRITING THIS BOOK, I had two things that I had to adhere to; impartiality and non-judgemental. This therefore was the only way to tell this complicated sad story without skewing the narrative to one direction.

The first few chapters of this book delves on "the blunt side of things" discussing the beginning of foreign interference and the taking over of Arab states from the Ottoman empire and the events that took place after this horrific experience. The middle part of the book discusses current Palestinian land rights and the struggles under the Ottoman and then the British and the creation of the Jewish state that witnessed almost a million Arabs being destituted and banished out of their homeland never to be allowed back again. The last part of this book covers the events that followed after the horrific incident of October 7th between HAMAS and Israel.

Pre-colonial Arab societies

PRE-COLONIAL ARAB SOCIETIES were characterised by a rich tapestry of culture, trade, and social organisation, existing long before the advent of European colonial powers. The Arabian Peninsula, with its diverse geography ranging from deserts to coastal regions, fostered a variety of communities, each with its own customs, languages, and systems of governance. These societies were often organised around tribal affiliations, with clans playing a significant role in social structure and political alliances. Trade routes, such as those connecting the Mediterranean with the Indian Ocean, facilitated not only economic exchanges but also cultural interactions, leading to the flourishing of cities like Mecca and Medina as centres of commerce and spirituality.

The arrival of Islam in the 7th century CE marked a significant turning point for Arab societies, unifying various tribes under a common religious framework while also establishing a vast empire that extended well beyond the Arabian Peninsula. This expansion facilitated the spread of Arabic culture and language, creating a shared identity among diverse groups across the Middle East and North Africa. The Islamic Golden Age that followed saw remarkable advancements in science, philosophy, and the arts, with scholars from the Arab world contributing significantly to global knowledge. This period of prosperity and cohesion laid the foundation for a complex socio-political landscape that would later be disrupted by external forces.

As European powers began to assert their influence in the 19th and early 20th centuries, the stability and unity of pre-colonial Arab societies faced unprecedented challenges. The interests of colonial powers, particularly Britain and France, led to direct interventions and a reconfiguration of existing political boundaries. These interventions were often justified by a perceived need to modernise or stabilise the region, but they frequently disregarded the intricate social and cultural realities of the local populations. The imposition of foreign rule not only disrupted traditional governance systems but also sowed seeds of division among communities that had coexisted for centuries.

The Sykes-Picot Agreement of 1916 epitomized the covert negotiations between European powers that fundamentally altered the political landscape of the Middle East. This secret arrangement divided the Ottoman Empire's Arab provinces into spheres of influence, disregarding the aspirations of the Arab people for self-determination. The arbitrary borders drawn by colonial powers often cut across ethnic and sectarian lines, leading to long-term tensions and conflicts that continue to resonate today. The legacy of Sykes-Picot has been a source of grievance, as many in the Arab world perceive it as a betrayal of their historical claims to land and

The Sykes-Picot Agreement of 1916 epitomised the European powers' disregard for Arab aspirations and national identities. This secret arrangement between Britain and France, with Russian assent, outlined the division of Ottoman territories into spheres of influence, effectively disregarding the existing cultural and historical ties within the region. The agreement's revelation sparked widespread outrage among Arabs, who had been led to believe that their support against the Ottoman Empire would result in independence and self-determination. Instead, the arbitrary borders drawn by colonial powers laid the groundwork for future conflicts, as they failed to reflect the complex realities of ethnic and sectarian affiliations.

The consequences of the Sykes-Picot Agreement and subsequent foreign interventions have had lasting effects on modern Arab conflicts. The borders created by European powers not only divided communities but also established states that struggled to foster a cohesive national identity. These artificial boundaries contributed to tensions that have led to civil wars, sectarian violence, and regional instability, as various groups vie for control and recognition. The legacy of colonialism continues to resonate today, with many contemporary conflicts in the Arab world rooted in the historical grievances and socio-political fractures established during this tumultuous period.

In conclusion, the impact of the Ottoman Empire and the subsequent actions of European powers have been instrumental in shaping the modern Arab world. The dissolution of the empire and the imposition of foreign-dictated borders contributed to a complex web of identity and conflict that continues to challenge the region. Understanding this historical context is essential for grasping the dynamics of current events and conflicts in the Arab world, where the echoes of past betrayals still reverberate through the political and social landscapes. The interplay of historical legacies and contemporary challenges highlights the need for a nuanced approach to addressing the region's ongoing struggles.

Chapter 2: European Interests in the Arab World

The Age of Imperialism

The Age of Imperialism marked a significant period in which European powers expanded their territories and influence across the globe, profoundly impacting regions such as the Arab world. From the late 19th century into the early 20th century, the scramble for colonies intensified, driven by industrialisation, nationalism, and a desire for new markets. European nations, particularly Britain and France, sought to exert control over vast territories in Africa and the Middle East, often disregarding the cultural and political realities of the regions they colonised. This imperialist ambition laid the groundwork for the eventual division of the Arab world, as European powers imposed borders that ignored the existing ethnic, tribal, and religious affiliations of the local populations.

The actions of European powers during this period were instrumental in shaping the modern Middle Eastern borders that we recognise today. The arbitrary lines drawn on maps often failed to consider the historical contexts and relationships among different groups. Instead, these borders were created to serve the strategic interests of the colonisers, facilitating easier administration and control. As a result, many of the states formed under colonial rule lacked the cohesion and legitimacy that are essential for stable governance. This disregard for indigenous governance structures created lasting tensions and conflicts that continue to plague the region.

One of the most significant agreements that exemplified the imperialist attitude towards the Arab world was the Sykes-Picot Agreement of 1916. Conceived in secrecy during World War I, this accord between Britain and France divided the Ottoman Empire's Arab territories into spheres of influence. The agreement promised to respect Arab aspirations for independence while simultaneously planning for the establishment of colonial mandates. The fallout from the Sykes-Picot Agreement was profound, as it cemented divisions that would later lead to national rivalries and conflict. The artificial boundaries drawn during this time did not reflect the aspirations of the Arab people, ultimately fuelling resentment and a sense of betrayal.

The consequences of foreign intervention during the Age of Imperialism have had lasting effects on modern Arab conflicts. The imposition of foreign powers disrupted established social and political systems, leading to instability that has persisted for decades. Many contemporary conflicts can trace their roots back to this era, as the legacies of imperialism continue to shape national identities and inter-state relations. The lack of genuine sovereignty and self-determination fostered a feeling of alienation among local populations, often resulting in resistance movements and uprisings against both colonial powers and their successors.

In conclusion, the Age of Imperialism was a critical juncture in the history of the Arab world, characterised by the intervention of European powers that fundamentally altered regional dynamics. The arbitrary borders established during this time, epitomised by agreements such as Sykes-Picot, not only disregarded the complexities of Arab identities but also set the stage for ongoing conflicts. Understanding this historical context is essential for comprehending the current challenges faced by the Arab world, as many of the issues stemming from this era continue to resonate in today's geopolitical landscape. The legacies of betrayal and division remain a crucial aspect of the narrative surrounding the Arab world and its relations with external powers.

Economic Motivations for Expansion

THE ECONOMIC MOTIVATIONS for expansion by European powers in the Arab world during the late 19th and early 20th centuries were driven by a complex interplay of factors, including the desire for resources, markets, and geopolitical dominance. As industrialisation progressed in Europe, the demands for raw materials such as oil, cotton, and minerals surged. The Arab regions, rich in these resources, became attractive targets for European nations seeking to fuel their growing economies. Control over these resources was not merely a matter of economic gain but also a strategic imperative to secure energy supplies and sustain military capabilities.

The establishment of colonial rule often coincided with the imposition of new economic structures in the Arab world. European powers restructured local economies to serve their interests, prioritising cash crops and resource extraction over traditional agricultural practices. The Sykes-Picot Agreement exemplified this shift, as it divided the Ottoman Empire's Arab territories into zones of influence between Britain and France. This division was not only a political manoeuvre but also an economic strategy, allowing these powers to monopolise trade routes and resource access, thereby enhancing their global economic positions.

Moreover, the creation of new borders often disrupted existing trade patterns and local economies. The arbitrary nature of these borders, drawn without regard for ethnic, tribal, or cultural affiliations, led to economic fragmentation. Regions that had previously enjoyed economic interdependence found themselves isolated by newly established national boundaries. This fragmentation fostered resentment and conflict, undermining the stability necessary for economic growth. The consequences of these divisions are still evident today, as many Arab nations struggle with the legacy of foreign-imposed boundaries that prioritise external economic interests over local needs.

European powers also recognised the potential for economic exploitation through political alliances with local leaders. By supporting certain groups over others, these powers could manipulate regional dynamics to their advantage, fostering divisions that served their economic goals. This tactic created a dependency on foreign powers, as local leaders sought military and financial support in exchange for access to resources. The resulting landscape was one where local economies became increasingly intertwined with the interests of foreign powers, complicating the prospects for independent economic development.

The long-term effects of these economic motivations for expansion are evident in modern Arab conflicts, where historical grievances related to resource control and economic inequality continue to fuel tensions. The legacy of foreign intervention has left a mark on the region, where the struggle for economic resources often translates into broader political and social conflicts.

Understanding the economic motivations behind the borders and divisions created by European powers is essential for comprehending the ongoing challenges faced by the Arab world today, as the echoes of past decisions continue to influence contemporary realities.

Strategic geopolitical considerations have played a pivotal role in the historical and contemporary shaping of the Arab world. Understanding the motivations and actions of European powers offers insights into how arbitrary borders were drawn, often with little regard for the cultural, ethnic, or religious identities of the people living in the region. The division of the Arab world by outsiders was not merely a product of colonial ambition; it was also a reflection of the strategic interests of European nations eager to secure resources, maintain influence, and counter rival powers. This complex interplay of interests laid the groundwork for a legacy of conflict and division that continues to resonate today.

The Sykes-Picot Agreement of 1916 serves as a prime example of how European powers manipulated the Arab world to suit their strategic needs. This secret accord between Britain and France, with Russian assent, effectively divided the Ottoman Empire's Arab territories into zones of influence, disregarding the aspirations of the Arab population for self-determination. The borders established by Sykes-Picot often split communities and ignored historical tribal and cultural affiliations. This disregard for local realities has had lasting consequences, contributing to an enduring sense of betrayal and resentment among Arab populations toward foreign powers and their imposed boundaries.

The consequences of the Sykes-Picot Agreement can be seen in the modern conflicts that plague the Arab world. The arbitrary borders drawn in the early 20th century have led to a patchwork of states that often lack cohesion and stability. Nations such as Iraq and Syria, whose borders were artificially constructed, have experienced significant internal strife as various ethnic and sectarian groups vie for power. Foreign intervention, often justified under the guise of promoting democracy or stability, has further exacerbated these tensions, leading to protracted conflicts that can be traced back to the historical decisions made by European powers.

Foreign intervention has not only shaped the geopolitical landscape but has also fuelled a cycle of violence and instability. The Iraq War, the Syrian civil war, and the Libyan conflict are all examples where external powers have intervened, often without a thorough understanding of the local dynamics. These interventions, frequently characterised by military action or political meddling, have led to significant humanitarian crises and created power vacuums that extremist groups have exploited. The ramifications of these conflicts have spread beyond the immediate region, affecting global security and prompting a revaluation of the West's role in the Middle East.

In conclusion, the strategic geopolitical considerations that shaped the Arab world during the colonial era continue to influence contemporary conflicts and relationships between nations. The legacy of the Sykes-Picot Agreement and subsequent foreign interventions highlights the complexities involved in nation-building and the necessity of understanding local contexts. As the Arab world grapples with the consequences of these historical decisions, it is essential for policymakers to recognise the importance of engaging with local populations and respecting their agency in shaping their futures, rather than imposing external solutions that may lead to further discord.

Chapter 3: The Sykes-Picot Agreement

Origins of the Agreement

The origins of the Sykes-Picot Agreement trace back to the geopolitical ambitions of European powers during World War I. As the Ottoman Empire crumbled under the pressures of the war, British and French officials sought to carve up its territories, particularly in the Middle East, to secure their own imperial interests. The discussions that led to this secret agreement began in 1915, when British diplomat Sir Mark Sykes and French diplomat François Georges-Picot were tasked with delineating spheres of influence in the region. Their negotiations were driven by a desire to control vital resources and trade routes, particularly in the context of a post-war world where the balance of power would shift dramatically.

The Sykes-Picot Agreement, finalised in May 1916, outlined the division of Ottoman lands into areas of direct and indirect control by Britain and France. The agreement proposed that the British would gain control over parts of modern-day Iraq, Jordan, and Palestine, while the French would oversee Syria and Lebanon. This partitioning disregarded the complex ethnic, religious, and cultural realities of the region, as it was primarily focused on meeting the strategic interests of the European powers rather than the aspirations of the local populations. The lack of consideration for the diverse communities in these territories would sow the seeds of future conflicts.

The consequences of the Sykes-Picot Agreement were profound and far-reaching. Upon the conclusion of World War I, the League of Nations mandates formalised the division of the Middle Eastern territories, often resulting in borders that split communities and ignored historical ties. The arbitrary lines drawn on the map not only created new nations but also set the stage for political instability, as they failed to account for the aspirations of Arabs who had been promised independence in exchange for their support against the Ottomans. Instead of fostering unity and self-determination, the agreement deepened divisions and led to a legacy of resentment toward foreign intervention.

The effects of foreign intervention in the Arab world became increasingly evident in the decades following the agreement. As Western powers continued to exert influence over the newly formed states, local governments struggled to establish legitimacy and stability. The imposition of foreign-backed regimes often led to authoritarian rule, exacerbating tensions within and between nations. The artificial borders created by the Sykes-Picot Agreement contributed to the rise of sectarian strife and nationalist movements, as marginalised groups sought to reclaim their identities and challenge the status quo imposed by external powers.

The legacy of the Sykes-Picot Agreement is still felt today, as the region grapples with the consequences of its origins. Modern conflicts in the Arab world frequently reflect the historical divisions created by this agreement and other imperial interventions. The ongoing struggles for power, autonomy, and recognition among various ethnic and religious groups can be traced back to the arbitrary borders established a century ago. As the region continues to navigate the complexities of its past, understanding the origins of such agreements is crucial to addressing the contemporary challenges faced by the Arab world.

Key figures involved

THE DIVISION OF THE Arab world and the manipulation of its borders by European powers were significantly influenced by key figures whose actions and decisions shaped the geopolitical landscape. Among these figures was Sir Mark Sykes, a British diplomat whose negotiations with French counterpart François Georges-Picot led to the infamous Sykes-Picot Agreement of 1916. This secret pact delineated spheres of influence in the Middle East and laid the groundwork for the modern borders of several Arab states. Sykes, motivated by imperial ambitions, viewed the Middle East primarily as a strategic asset for Britain, disregarding the historical, cultural, and social realities of the Arab populations. His role epitomised the broader colonial mindset that prioritised European interests over local identities.

On the French side, Georges-Picot played a crucial role in the negotiations that divided the Ottoman Empire's Arab territories. His vision aligned closely with French interests in expanding influence in the region, particularly in Syria and Lebanon. The agreement not only neglected the aspirations of Arab nationalism but also sowed seeds of discord among the various ethnic and religious groups. Picot's willingness to compromise the future of millions for the sake of French imperial expansion illustrated the extent to which European powers prioritised their geopolitical ambitions over the rights of the local populations. His contributions to the agreement left a lasting legacy of conflict and division in the Middle East.

Another pivotal figure was T.E. Lawrence, known as Lawrence of Arabia, whose involvement during World War I significantly shaped British policy towards the Arab Revolt. Lawrence advocated for Arab independence and played a key role in rallying Arab forces against Ottoman rule. His romanticised vision of a united Arab nation was, however, juxtaposed against the realities of European diplomacy, which ultimately undermined those aspirations. Lawrence's experiences and writings highlighted the complexities of the Arab struggle for self-determination, illustrating the tension between the aspirations of the Arab leaders and the duplicity of their European allies.

In addition to these figures, the impact of foreign intervention leaders such as U.S. President Woodrow Wilson cannot be overlooked. Wilson's Fourteen Points, which included principles of self-determination, initially inspired Arab leaders who hoped for post-war independence. However, the subsequent actions taken by Western powers, including the establishment of mandates and protectorates, revealed a stark contrast between rhetoric and reality. Wilson's ideals were often sacrificed at the altar of political expediency, leading to disillusionment within the Arab world and fuelling resentment towards Western influence.

The confluence of these key figures and their actions underscores the complexities of foreign intervention in the Arab world. The Sykes-Picot Agreement and its ramifications exemplify how decisions made in distant capitals profoundly affected the lives of millions. The legacy of these interventions continues to resonate in modern Arab conflicts, where historical grievances and arbitrary borders contribute to ongoing instability. Understanding the roles of these figures is essential to grasping the intricate dynamics of Arab history and the enduring consequences of colonialism in shaping contemporary Middle Eastern geopolitics.

Territorial divisions and their rationale

THE TERRITORIAL DIVISIONS within the Arab world have been a significant consequence of European colonial ambitions, particularly during the late 19th and early 20th centuries. These divisions were not merely a product of arbitrary decisions but rather a calculated approach by European powers to exert control over vast regions. The rationale behind these divisions was primarily driven by strategic interests, economic exploitation, and the desire to maintain influence over key trade routes and resources. The resulting borders often ignored the complex social, ethnic, and religious landscapes of the region, leading to long-term instability and conflict.

The Sykes-Picot Agreement of 1916, a secret accord between Britain and France. was aimed to divide the Ottoman Empire's Arab provinces into spheres of influence. The rationale behind Sykes-Picot was to secure British and French interests in the region ahead of the anticipated downfall of Ottoman control. The lines drawn on the map disregarded existing tribal and cultural affiliations, creating a patchwork of states that would struggle with national identity and governance. The lack of consideration for local dynamics has had enduring consequences, contributing to conflict and fragmentation in the Arab world.

The post-World War I mandates established by the League of Nations further solidified the territorial divisions initiated by Sykes-Picot. European powers, particularly Britain and France, were given administrative control over various territories, ostensibly to prepare them for self-governance. However, the rationale for these mandates was often steeped in a paternalistic view that the Arab populations were not ready for independence. This foreign intervention not only delayed the development of national identities but also entrenched colonial powers in the region, fostering resentment and anti-colonial sentiment that would erupt in various forms of resistance and conflict.

The consequences of these imposed borders and foreign interventions have been profound and far-reaching. In the decades following the establishment of these artificial states, the Arab world has experienced a series of conflicts, civil wars, and power struggles, often exacerbated by external influences. The legacy of colonialism is evident in the ongoing political instability and sectarian violence that characterise many Arab countries today. The divisions created by European powers have led to fragmented national identities, where loyalty to ethnic or sectarian groups often supersedes allegiance to the state.

In conclusion, the territorial divisions within the Arab world represent a complex interplay of colonial ambition and geopolitical strategy. The decisions made by European powers during the early 20th century have had lasting impacts, resulting in a landscape marked by conflict and division. Understanding the rationale behind these divisions is crucial for addressing the contemporary challenges faced by the region. As modern conflicts continue to unfold, the historical context of foreign intervention and imposed borders remains a critical factor in the search for stability and peace in the Arab world.

Chapter 4: Consequences of the Sykes-Picot agreement

Redrawing Borders and Creating States
The redrawing of borders and the creation of new states in the Arab world were primarily influenced by European powers during the late 19th and early 20th centuries. This process was not merely a matter of geographic realignment; it represented a fundamental reshaping of identities, cultures, and political landscapes across the region. The decline of the Ottoman Empire presented European nations with an opportunity to exert their influence and control in the Middle East. Consequently, the arbitrary borders drawn by foreign powers disregarded the historical, ethnic, and religious complexities of the region, leading to long-term consequences that resonate to this day.

The consequences of these artificially imposed borders have manifested in various ways, contributing to enduring conflicts and instability. Many of the newly formed states struggled with internal divisions, as diverse groups found themselves placed within the same national framework. This lack of cohesion has often led to civil strife, sectarian violence, and, in some cases, the emergence of extremist movements. The inability of these states to foster a unifying national identity has perpetuated a cycle of conflict, undermining the prospects for peace and development.

Furthermore, foreign intervention in the Arab world has continued to shape the dynamics of conflict and governance. The legacies of colonialism are evident in contemporary issues, where foreign powers have often intervened in local conflicts to further their strategic interests. The Gulf War, the Iraq War, and the ongoing Syrian civil war exemplify how external actors can exacerbate existing tensions rather than resolve them. The involvement of foreign powers has frequently led to the fragmentation of states and the rise of non-state actors, complicating the path to stability and governance in the region.

In conclusion, the redrawing of borders and the creation of states in the Arab world by European powers were underpinned by a disregard for the intricate social fabric of the region. The Sykes-Picot Agreement serves as a historical marker of how foreign interests can dictate national boundaries, often with catastrophic consequences. The ongoing repercussions of these actions are evident in the modern conflicts that plague the region, highlighting the importance of understanding this historical context. Only by acknowledging the complexities of these early decisions can one begin to grasp the challenges faced by the Arab world today.

The birth of nationalism and resistance

THE BIRTH OF NATIONALISM in the Arab world can be traced back to the late 19th and early 20th centuries, a period marked by the decline of the Ottoman Empire and the encroachment of European powers in the region. As the Ottomans weakened, the idea of a distinct Arab identity began to take shape, fuelled by a growing awareness of shared language, culture, and history among various Arab communities. This burgeoning nationalism was often in response to external pressures, particularly from European colonial interests that sought to exploit the region's resources and geopolitical significance. Nationalist movements began to emerge, advocating for self-determination and the establishment of sovereign Arab states, which were often viewed as a means to resist foreign domination.

Foreign intervention in the Arab world has had lasting effects on modern conflicts, often exacerbating divisions and tensions within states. The imposition of Western political structures and economic systems frequently undermined traditional governance and social cohesion, leading to instability and violence. In many cases, external powers continued to manipulate local politics to serve their interests, supporting authoritarian regimes or engaging in military interventions that further fuelled resistance movements. The legacy of colonialism, coupled with ongoing foreign involvement, has created a complex landscape of conflict in which nationalism and the desire for sovereignty often clash with external influences.

In conclusion, the birth of nationalism in the Arab world is deeply intertwined with the actions of European powers that sought to reshape the region for their own purposes. The arbitrary borders established through agreements like Sykes-Picot not only disregarded the realities of Arab identity but also sowed the seeds of ongoing conflict and resistance. As the Arab nations grapple with the consequences of this historical betrayal, the struggle for self-determination and the quest for national identity remain central themes in the contemporary socio-political landscape. Understanding this interplay between nationalism and foreign intervention is crucial to grasping the complexities of modern Arab conflicts and the enduring impact of historical decisions made long ago.

Long-term political and social implications

FOREIGN INTERVENTION has not only created immediate political ramifications but has also exacerbated social issues within Arab societies. The imposition of Western-style governance systems often clashed with traditional forms of authority, leading to a crisis of legitimacy for many regimes. As a result, the state-building efforts initiated by foreign powers frequently resulted in weak institutions that struggled to address the needs of their citizens. This disconnection has fuelled widespread disenchantment, contributing to the rise of extremist groups that exploit grievances against both local governments and foreign influences. Consequently, the socio-political landscape of the Arab world has been marked by violence, instability, and the emergence of non-state actors.

The ramifications of these historical decisions are evident in the ongoing conflicts that plague the region. Civil wars, insurgencies, and the rise of terrorist organisations can often be traced back to the legacy of European colonialism and the subsequent geopolitical manoeuvring during the Cold War and beyond. These conflicts have further fragmented societies and deepened sectarian divides, as groups vie for power and recognition within states that lack cohesive national identities. The international community's response to these crises, often characterised by military intervention or diplomatic neglect, has failed to resolve the underlying issues rooted in the historical context of foreign domination.

In conclusion, the long-term political and social implications of European powers in the Arab world serve as a critical reminder of the importance of understanding historical contexts in analysing contemporary issues. The arbitrary borders, the imposition of foreign governance models, and the failure to address the aspirations of local populations have created a landscape marked by conflict and division. As the Arab world continues to grapple with the consequences of these interventions, it becomes increasingly essential for both regional leaders and international actors to engage with history thoughtfully, aiming for solutions that recognise the complexities of identity, governance, and social cohesion in the quest for peace and stability.

Chapter 5: The role of foreign intervention in modern conflicts

Case studies: Iraq, Syria, and Libya

The case studies of Iraq, Syria, and Libya offer critical insights into how European powers have influenced the political landscape of the Arab world, often leading to divisions that have had lasting consequences. Each of these countries reflects the complex interplay of colonial ambitions, geopolitical strategies, and the repercussions of arbitrary borders drawn by foreign powers. The legacy of the Sykes-Picot Agreement, which partitioned the Ottoman Empire's Arab provinces during World War I, is particularly evident in these nations, where artificial borders have often disregarded ethnic, religious, and cultural realities.

In Iraq, the borders established by European powers created a state that encompassed diverse ethnic and sectarian groups, including Arabs, Kurds, and Turkmen, as well as Sunni and Shia Muslims. The imposition of these borders ignored longstanding rivalries and historical grievances, leading to periodic conflicts and tensions. The aftermath of the 2003 invasion by the United States, a move supported by several European nations, further destabilised the country, leading to the rise of extremist groups like ISIS. The foreign intervention not only exacerbated existing divisions but also introduced new complexities, demonstrating how external influences can disrupt the fragile balance within a nation.

Syria's experience mirrors that of Iraq, with the civil war that erupted in 2011 serving as a stark example of how foreign intervention can complicate internal conflicts. The initial protests against the Assad regime were met with violent repression, leading to a multifaceted civil war involving various domestic and international actors. European powers, alongside the United

States and Russia, became embroiled in the conflict, supporting different factions based on their geopolitical interests. This foreign involvement has perpetuated a cycle of violence and instability, with the borders of Syria once again being contested by both state and non-state actors.

Libya's case further illustrates the consequences of foreign intervention, particularly following the NATO-led military intervention in 2011 that resulted in the overthrow of Muammar Gaddafi. While the intervention was initially justified as a means to protect civilians, it ultimately led to a power vacuum and a protracted civil conflict among rival factions. The absence of a coherent post-Gaddafi governance structure, coupled with ongoing foreign backers seeking to influence the outcome, has left Libya fragmented and struggling with lawlessness. The legacy of colonial interventions is evident in the ongoing struggles for power and legitimacy among various groups within the country.

Collectively, these case studies highlight the profound impact of European powers on the shaping of the Arab world. The arbitrary borders drawn through agreements like Sykes-Picot have created a legacy of division and conflict that continues to resonate today. Foreign interventions, often motivated by geopolitical interests, have further complicated these dynamics, resulting in instability that undermines the prospects for peace and reconciliation. Understanding these historical contexts is essential for grasping the contemporary challenges facing Iraq, Syria, and Libya, as well as the broader implications for the region as a whole.

The influence of Western powers

THE INFLUENCE OF WESTERN powers on the Arab world has been profound, particularly during the late 19th and early 20th centuries. This period marked a significant shift in the political landscape of the Middle East, as European nations sought to expand their empires and exert control over the region. The motivations behind this intervention were often rooted in economic interests, strategic advantages, and a desire to impose Western ideologies. As Western powers carved up territories, the consequences of their actions set the stage for enduring conflicts and divisions that continue to affect the region today.

The aftermath of the Sykes-Picot Agreement had far-reaching consequences for the newly formed states in the Middle East. The imposition of Western-drawn borders led to a series of conflicts, as various communities struggled for power and recognition within their respective nations. In countries like Iraq, Syria, and Lebanon, the legacy of colonial boundaries continues to manifest in sectarian strife and political instability. The arbitrary nature of these borders has often been cited as a primary factor in the region's cycles of violence and unrest, as populations grapple with identities that do not align with the imposed national frameworks.

Foreign intervention in the Arab world did not cease with the establishment of new borders; rather, it evolved into a more direct involvement in regional conflicts. Throughout the 20th and into the 21st century, Western powers have engaged in military interventions, support for various factions, and diplomatic manoeuvring that have further complicated the dynamics of the region. The invasions of Iraq in 2003 and Libya in 2011 highlight how foreign powers often prioritize strategic interests over the stability of local populations. These interventions have led to power vacuums, the rise of extremist groups, and continued humanitarian crises.

The influence of Western powers on the Arab world exemplifies how external forces can shape the destinies of nations and communities. The historical decisions made by European powers not only altered the geopolitical landscape but also created a legacy of mistrust and conflict that persists today. Understanding the ramifications of these influences is crucial for comprehending the complexities of modern Arab conflicts and the ongoing struggle for identity, sovereignty, and peace in the region.

Regional responses and repercussions

THE DIVISION OF THE Arab world by European powers has roots that extend deep into the colonial ambitions of the late 19th and early 20th centuries. As European nations sought to expand their empires, they turned their attention to the Middle East, an area rich in resources and strategically significant. The arbitrary borders drawn during this period disregarded the historical, tribal, and cultural affiliations of the region's inhabitants. This process not only fostered a sense of dislocation among the Arab populations but also laid the groundwork for future conflicts, as newly created states found themselves struggling with internal divisions that had been ignored by their colonizers.

The foreign intervention in the Arab world did not cease with the end of colonial mandates; rather, it evolved into a pattern of involvement in modern conflicts. The Gulf Wars, the Syrian civil war, and the rise of extremist groups can all be traced back to the historical interventions and decisions made by European powers and later the United States. These conflicts revealed the fragility of the states created through foreign imposition, as the lack of cohesive national identities made it difficult for these countries to navigate the challenges posed by internal divisions and external pressures. The ongoing violence and instability serve as a stark reminder of the long-lasting impacts of colonialism in the region.

Today, the repercussions of these historical decisions continue to shape the Arab world, as nations grapple with the legacies of imposed borders and foreign intervention. The Arab Spring, while initially a movement for democratic reform, revealed deep-seated grievances rooted in the historical context of colonial rule and its aftermath. As countries struggle to forge national identities that reflect their diverse populations, the shadow of the past looms large, complicating efforts toward unity and stability. Understanding these regional responses and the historical context of foreign intervention is essential for comprehending the complexities of modern conflicts in the Arab world.

Cultural and social disruption

CULTURAL AND SOCIAL disruption in the Arab world has roots that extend deep into the history of European intervention and colonialism. The arbitrary drawing of borders by foreign powers, often disregarding existing ethnic, tribal, and sectarian lines, initiated a cascade of fragmentation that would transform societies across the region. Historically, the Arab world consisted of diverse groups with intricate social structures, but the imposition of new national identities and political boundaries shattered traditional ties. This disruption was not merely geographical; it also eroded communal bonds and instigated conflicts that continue to resonate today.

Foreign intervention exacerbated the challenges faced by the newly formed Arab states. As European powers continued to meddle in the region's affairs, their involvement often prioritised strategic interests over the well-being of local populations. The support of certain regimes or factions led to a cycle of dependency, where local leaders relied on external powers for legitimacy and security. This dynamic not only undermined sovereignty but also fostered resentment among marginalised groups, further complicating social cohesion and leading to violent uprisings in various countries.

The impact of cultural disruption is evident in the rise of radical ideologies and extremist groups that have exploited the vacuum created by weakened state structures. In many cases, these groups emerged as alternative sources of identity and belonging in a landscape marked by disillusionment with traditional governance. The power struggles spurred by foreign interventions have allowed such movements to gain traction, drawing on the grievances of disaffected populations who feel abandoned by both their leaders and the international community. This has resulted in conflicts that are frequently portrayed as religious or ideological battles, obscuring the underlying social and political issues rooted in historical grievances.

Ultimately, the cultural and social disruption in the Arab world reflects the long-lasting consequences of external manipulation and control. The arbitrary borders established by European powers not only divided communities but also stifled the organic development of national identities. As the region grapples with the repercussions of this historical legacy, it is essential to acknowledge the role of foreign powers in shaping the socio-political landscape. Understanding these dynamics is crucial for any meaningful dialogue about the future of the Arab world and the pursuit of stability and peace in the region.

Economic dependencies

ECONOMIC DEPENDENCIES have played a crucial role in shaping the political landscape of the Arab world, particularly in the context of European powers' interventions. From the late 19th century onward, European nations sought to expand their influence in the Middle East, often through economic means. This was driven by the region's vast natural resources, strategic trade routes, and the desire to establish markets for European goods. The imposition of economic structures designed to benefit the colonisers laid the groundwork for a dependence that would have lasting implications for the newly formed states after the fall of empires.

The Sykes-Picot Agreement of 1916, which divided the Ottoman Empire's Arab territories between British and French control, exemplifies how economic interests dictated political decisions. By creating arbitrary borders that ignored ethnic and sectarian realities, the agreement facilitated the extraction of resources and control of trade routes. The resulting economic dependencies were not merely a byproduct of colonialism but a deliberate strategy to ensure that newly established states remained reliant on their former colonisers for trade, investment, and even governance. This legacy of dependency has continued to shape economic relations in the region, often leading to instability and conflict.

In the post-colonial era, foreign intervention has further entrenched these economic dependencies, with external powers continuing to exert influence over Arab economies. Countries like the United States and various European states have often pursued policies that favoured their economic interests, manipulating local economies to serve foreign agendas. This has manifested in various forms, such as arms sales, military aid, and economic partnerships that prioritise foreign profit over local development. The result is a cycle of dependency where Arab nations struggle to assert economic autonomy, often resulting in political and social unrest.

Moreover, the consequences of these economic dependencies have been exacerbated by ongoing conflicts in the region. The presence of foreign powers, under the guise of humanitarian assistance or stabilisation efforts, frequently leads to the perpetuation of dependency rather than fostering genuine economic independence. In many cases, the influx of foreign aid and investment has not translated into sustainable economic growth but has instead created a landscape where local economies are fragile and heavily influenced by external actors. This dynamic complicates the quest for stability and peace, as local entities become embroiled in a complex web of obligations to foreign interests.

Ultimately, the economic dependencies established by European powers and perpetuated by ongoing foreign interventions have profoundly influenced the political and social fabric of the Arab world. The arbitrary borders drawn in the early 20th century, combined with the legacy of colonial economic structures, have created a dependency that hinders the region's ability to navigate its own future. Understanding these economic relationships is essential for comprehending the broader narrative of conflict, national identity, and the struggle for sovereignty in the contemporary Arab world.

The rise of authoritarian regimes

THE RISE OF AUTHORITARIAN regimes in the Arab world can be traced back to the geopolitical machinations of European powers in the early 20th century, particularly following World War I. The imposition of arbitrary borders, largely defined by the Sykes-Picot Agreement of 1916, created nations that lacked cohesive national identities. These borders often split ethnic and religious groups, fostering tensions that would later be exploited by authoritarian leaders. As these regimes emerged, they capitalised on the fragmented national identities, promoting a narrative of unity and strength against perceived external threats, which often included the very powers that had drawn the borders.

The Sykes-Picot Agreement and its aftermath fundamentally altered the political landscape of the Middle East. The artificial boundaries established by this agreement led to the creation of new states that were ill-equipped to govern themselves effectively. Consequently, many of these newly formed nations fell under the control of authoritarian rulers who promised stability and order in the face of chaos, often at the expense of democratic governance and civil liberties.

Foreign intervention has played a crucial role in reinforcing authoritarian regimes throughout the Arab world. In many cases, external powers supported dictatorial leaders who aligned with their strategic interests, providing military and financial assistance that helped entrench these regimes. This support often came with a disregard for the democratic aspirations of the populace, leading to widespread disenchantment and unrest. The consequences of such interventions were profound, as they not only bolstered authoritarianism but also contributed to cycles of violence and instability, further complicating the region's political landscape.

The consequences of authoritarian rule in the Arab world have been far-reaching, leading to widespread human rights abuses, economic stagnation, and social unrest. These regimes frequently suppressed dissent through censorship, imprisonment, and violence, creating a climate of fear that stifled political engagement and reform. As citizens became increasingly disillusioned, the lack of legitimate political avenues often pushed them towards radicalisation or rebellion, resulting in the emergence of extremist groups that exploited the vacuum left by weak or corrupt states. This dynamic has contributed to ongoing conflicts, further entrenching the power of authoritarian leaders who claim to be the only viable alternative to chaos.

In summary, the rise of authoritarian regimes in the Arab world is intricately linked to the historical actions of European powers and their reconfiguration of the region's political landscape. The legacy of the Sykes-Picot Agreement and subsequent foreign interventions fostered an environment where authoritarianism could thrive. These regimes, born of external imposition rather than genuine national identity, have perpetuated cycles of oppression and conflict, leaving a lasting impact on the Arab world. Understanding this context is essential for comprehending the complexities of contemporary Arab politics and the struggles faced by those seeking democratic governance and social justice.

Chapter 6: Reassessing borders and identities

Contemporary movements for change

Contemporary movements for change within the Arab world are deeply rooted in historical grievances stemming from the arbitrary borders established by European powers. The legacy of colonialism is evident in the political, social, and economic challenges faced by many Arab nations today. The imposition of borders without regard for ethnic, tribal, or sectarian lines has led to persistent conflicts and a struggle for identity among the populations. These movements seek to address the fragmentation and dislocation caused by foreign interventions, advocating for a re-examination of national identities that are more inclusive and representative of the diverse populations within these borders.

A significant aspect of contemporary movements for change is the widespread demand for political reform and increased democratic governance. Many Arab citizens are advocating for systems that reflect their aspirations for freedom and dignity, as seen in the Arab Spring uprisings that began in 2010. These movements were fuelled by frustration over authoritarian regimes, economic hardship, and perceived injustices rooted in both local governance and the historical imposition of foreign powers. The desire for a new social contract that prioritises citizen rights and accountability has become a cornerstone of contemporary activism, challenging the status quo established during the colonial period and perpetuated by subsequent regimes.

Moreover, the Sykes-Picot Agreement remains a focal point of criticism among those advocating for change. This agreement, which divided the Ottoman Empire's Arab territories into spheres of influence for Britain and France, is often cited as a symbol of Western betrayal and manipulation. Contemporary movements highlight the need to reassess these boundaries to foster unity among various groups that share cultural and historical ties.

Activists argue that the arbitrary nature of these borders has not only led to conflict but has also stifled potential cooperation and development across the region. By reimagining these divisions, contemporary movements aim to create a more cohesive and peaceful Arab world.

The role of foreign intervention in modern Arab conflicts continues to be a significant motivator for change. From military interventions to economic sanctions, the actions of external powers have often exacerbated existing tensions rather than resolving them. Movements for change argue for a rejection of foreign meddling and a call for self-determination, emphasising that true progress can only come from within. The emphasis on sovereignty and local agency is a response to a history of exploitation and manipulation, and contemporary activists are increasingly vocal in demanding that their voices be heard in discussions about their futures.

Finally, the emergence of digital activism has transformed the landscape of contemporary movements for change in the Arab world. Social media platforms have provided a space for grassroots organising and the dissemination of information, allowing activists to connect across borders and mobilise support for their causes. This digital revolution has not only amplified local voices but has also attracted international attention to the struggles faced by various communities. By leveraging technology, contemporary movements are able to challenge the narratives imposed by foreign powers and articulate their visions for a more just and equitable society, rooted in their own histories and aspirations.

The Quest for unity in diversity

THE QUEST FOR UNITY in diversity within the Arab world is intrinsically tied to the historical context of how its nations were shaped by external forces, particularly European powers. The arbitrary borders drawn during the colonial era often disregarded ethnic, cultural, and sectarian identities, leading to divisions that persist to this day. This artificial delineation created a patchwork of nations often at odds with one another, fostering an environment ripe for conflict. Understanding this quest for unity requires an exploration of the historical decisions made by foreign powers that prioritised their interests over the aspirations of the Arab people.

The arbitrary nature of the borders established by European powers has led to a complex tapestry of identities within the Arab world. Ethnic groups such as Kurds, Arabs, and Berbers, along with various religious sects, were often grouped together or separated without consideration for their historical connections. This lack of cultural cohesion has fuelled tensions, leading to civil strife and the rise of extremist factions that exploit these divisions. Furthermore, the promotion of nationalist movements by colonial powers often exacerbated internal divisions, as competing interests clashed in the pursuit of statehood and identity.

In the wake of decolonisation, the Arab world has struggled to reconcile its diverse identities with the need for national unity. The quest for unity in diversity has been challenged by ongoing foreign interventions that have often aimed to exploit these divisions for geopolitical gain. Whether through military intervention, economic support for certain factions, or the promotion of external political agendas, foreign powers have continually influenced the dynamics of Arab societies, sometimes exacerbating existing tensions rather than fostering reconciliation and unity.

Ultimately, the quest for unity in diversity within the Arab world is a reflection of a broader struggle to reclaim agency over its own destiny. The legacy of European powers in shaping borders and influencing internal politics has left a complicated inheritance. As contemporary Arab nations navigate the complexities of their identities, the path toward unity lies in acknowledging the diversity within their borders while fostering dialogue and cooperation. This journey is essential not only for the stability of the region but also for the empowerment of its people to forge a collective identity that honours their shared history and aspirations.

Future prospects for the Arab world

THE FUTURE PROSPECTS for the Arab world are shaped by a complex interplay of historical legacies, ongoing conflicts, and emerging geopolitical dynamics. The division of the Arab world by foreign powers has left a lasting impact on national identities, political stability, and regional cooperation. As the Arab nations navigate their contemporary challenges, the lingering effects of colonial interventions and arbitrary borders created by European powers continue to influence political discourse and social cohesion. The quest for national sovereignty and identity remains central to the aspirations of many Arab states, as they seek to reconcile their historical grievances with the demands of modern governance and international relations.

British and French spheres of influence, not only established borders that often disregarded ethnic and sectarian realities but also fostered a legacy of mistrust and discord among Arab populations. As nations grapple with the arbitrary nature of their borders, the challenge of fostering national unity amidst diverse identities has become increasingly pertinent. The future of the Arab world will heavily depend on the ability of its leaders to address these divisions while promoting inclusive governance and social cohesion.

Foreign intervention has played a significant role in shaping modern Arab conflicts, often exacerbating existing tensions and complicating efforts toward resolution. The myriads of external influences—from military interventions to economic sanctions—has frequently undermined local governance structures, leading to prolonged instability. In this context, the future of the Arab world hinges on establishing a framework for regional security that prioritises the sovereignty of Arab nations and fosters collaboration rather than competition. Effective diplomacy and multilateral engagement will be essential in addressing the root causes of conflict and promoting sustainable peace in the region.

In recent years, there has been a notable shift in how some Arab nations are approaching their international relationships, particularly with emerging powers such as China and Russia. This diversification of alliances presents both opportunities and challenges, as countries seek to balance their historical ties with Western powers against the backdrop of evolving global dynamics. The future prospects for the Arab world will likely be influenced by how effectively these nations can leverage new partnerships while ensuring that their domestic agendas remain cantered on development, human rights, and social justice.

Finally, the role of civil society and grassroots movements cannot be overlooked when considering the future of the Arab world. These groups are increasingly advocating for political reform, economic opportunity, and social equity, reflecting the aspirations of younger generations eager for change. The success of these movements will be crucial in shaping the political landscape and ensuring that the voices of the populace are heard in decision-making processes. As the Arab world confronts its past and envisions its future, the interplay between external influences, national sovereignty, and the agency of its citizens will ultimately determine the trajectory of the region in the years to come.

Chapter 7: Conclusion: lessons from history

Understanding the roots of conflict

The roots of conflict within the Arab world can be traced back to a series of historical events and decisions made by foreign powers, particularly European nations, during the late 19th and early 20th centuries. The decline of the Ottoman Empire created a power vacuum in the region, prompting European powers to exert influence over Arab territories. This period marked the beginning of a complex interplay of colonial ambitions, nationalist movements, and the imposition of arbitrary borders that would sow the seeds of future discord. As European powers sought to expand their empires, they often overlooked the cultural, ethnic, and religious complexities of the regions they occupied, leading to divisions that continue to resonate in contemporary conflicts.

The consequences of the Sykes-Picot Agreement were profound and far-reaching. It contributed to the creation of modern nation-states in the Arab world, many of which were unable to develop cohesive national identities due to the imposed divisions. The lack of consideration for local governance and the prioritisation of European interests destabilised the region, leading to a legacy of authoritarian regimes that often-suppressed dissent. These artificial borders have also facilitated the rise of sectarian tensions, as groups that had coexisted for centuries found themselves divided by newly drawn lines, leading to a cycle of violence and retribution that persists today.

Foreign intervention in the Middle East has further exacerbated these conflicts, often resulting in the destabilisation of governments and the rise of extremist groups. From the Cold War era to the present day, various powers have intervened militarily and politically, driven by strategic interests rather than the welfare of the local populations. These interventions have often been justified under the guise of promoting democracy or stability, yet they have frequently led to unintended consequences, including civil wars, refugee crises, and the emergence of terrorism. The continuous cycle of foreign involvement has perpetuated a sense of distrust among Arab nations towards external actors, complicating efforts toward peace and reconciliation.

Understanding the roots of conflict in the Arab world requires a critical examination of the historical decisions made by foreign powers, particularly those of European nations. The legacy of the Sykes-Picot Agreement and subsequent interventions has left a deep imprint on the political and social fabric of the region. As the Arab world grapples with the consequences of these historical actions, it is essential to acknowledge the complexities involved and the need for a nuanced approach to conflict resolution that respects the voices and aspirations of the people in the region. Only by confronting the historical injustices can there be hope for a more stable and peaceful future in the Arab world.

The importance of sovereignty and self-determination

THE CONCEPTS OF SOVEREIGNTY and self-determination are critical in understanding the historical and contemporary dynamics of the Arab world, especially in the context of European powers' influence. Sovereignty refers to the authority of a state to govern itself without external interference, while self-determination is the right of peoples to determine their political status and pursue their economic, social, and cultural development. These principles were systematically undermined during the colonial era, particularly with the arbitrary borders drawn by European powers, which disregarded the ethnic, tribal, and religious identities of the Arab populations. The consequences of this disregard continue to resonate throughout the region today.

The division of the Arab world by outsiders was marked by the imposition of artificial boundaries that often split communities and created tensions. The Sykes-Picot Agreement of 1916 exemplifies this trend. Conceived in secrecy between Britain and France, this agreement aimed to delineate spheres of influence in the Middle East following the anticipated collapse of the Ottoman Empire. The resulting borders ignored historical affiliations and local governance structures, laying the groundwork for future conflicts and instability. As a consequence, many Arab populations found themselves governed by foreign-imposed authorities that lacked legitimacy in the eyes of the local populace.

Furthermore, the ramifications of the Sykes-Picot Agreement extend beyond mere geographic divisions; they have fostered a legacy of conflict and resistance against perceived foreign domination. The arbitrary borders created by European powers not only led to political fragmentation but also contributed to the rise of nationalist movements seeking to reclaim sovereignty and assert self-determination. The Arab world became a stage for various ideological and political struggles, as groups sought to challenge the existing power structures that had been imposed upon them. This struggle for sovereignty remains a central theme in the region's modern conflicts.

Foreign intervention in Arab states has often exacerbated these challenges. Outside powers have frequently intervened in local conflicts, further complicating the pursuit of self-determination. From military interventions to economic sanctions, these foreign actions have often prioritised the interests of external actors over the aspirations of local populations. The resulting instability has perpetuated cycles of violence and unrest, undermining the sovereignty of nations that are still grappling with the consequences of colonial legacies and foreign meddling. As a result, the quest for sovereignty and self-determination continues to be a vital issue for many Arab societies.

Ultimately, the importance of sovereignty and self-determination cannot be overstated in the context of the Arab world. The historical experiences of colonisation and the ongoing effects of foreign intervention have created a complex landscape where the struggle for genuine autonomy remains paramount. Understanding these dynamics is essential for anyone seeking to grasp the intricacies of modern Middle Eastern conflicts and the enduring quest for political legitimacy and national identity in a region shaped by the borders of betrayal.

The historical narrative of the Arab world is profoundly intertwined with the interventions of European powers, whose actions have significantly shaped the political landscape of the region. Moving towards a collaborative future necessitates a critical understanding of how these external influences have contributed to the division and fragmentation of Arab nations. From the late 19th century into the 20th century, the ambitions of European states often eclipsed the aspirations of local populations, leading to arbitrary borders that disregarded ethnic, religious, and cultural affiliations. This legacy of division has created deep-seated tensions that persist today, underscoring the necessity for a collaborative approach to address historical grievances and promote unity.

The arbitrary nature of these borders has not only led to political instability but has also contributed to a sense of betrayal among Arab populations, who felt sidelined in their quest for self-determination. Recognising the implications of such historical agreements is crucial for fostering dialogue and cooperation, as it allows for a re-examination of national identities that have been shaped by external forces.

In examining the role of foreign intervention in contemporary Arab conflicts, it becomes evident that the patterns established in the past continue to influence present-day dynamics. The influx of foreign military and economic support has often exacerbated existing divisions, rather than facilitating resolution. As various factions vie for power, the involvement of external actors has complicated the landscape, leading to a cycle of dependency and conflict. To move toward a collaborative future, it is essential to prioritise local agency and empower communities to shape their own destinies, rather than imposing external solutions that may not resonate with the realities on the ground.

A collaborative future for the Arab world also necessitates a concerted effort to build relationships among nations and foster regional integration. This approach can be informed by historical lessons, emphasising the importance of solidarity and mutual respect among Arab states. Initiatives that promote economic cooperation, cultural exchange, and shared governance can help to bridge divides created by historical grievances and external interventions. Furthermore, fostering dialogue among diverse groups within the Arab world will enhance understanding and pave the way for collective problem-solving, ultimately leading to more sustainable peace and stability.

As the Arab world confronts the legacies of the past, embracing a collaborative future is not only a possibility but a necessity for overcoming historical betrayals. By acknowledging the role of European powers in shaping regional dynamics, addressing the consequences of agreements like Sykes-Picot, and critically evaluating foreign interventions, the region can embark on a path that prioritises unity and collaboration. Building on the foundation of shared history and common interests, the Arab world has the potential to redefine its identity and pursue a future marked by cooperation, resilience, and mutual respect.

Chapter 8: Introduction to Palestinian land rights

The historical context of Palestinian land ownership is complex and marked by various socio-political changes over centuries. Before the onset of the 20th century, the region known today as Palestine was characterised by a diverse population that included Muslims, Christians, and Jews, all of whom had long-standing ties to the land. The Ottoman Empire governed the area until the end of World War I, during which time land ownership was often communal rather than individual. This communal approach created a strong sense of local identity tied to the land, which is crucial for understanding the subsequent displacement and land loss that many Palestinians would face.

The transition from Ottoman to British control in 1917 introduced new legal frameworks and land policies that favoured Jewish immigration and land acquisition. The Balfour Declaration of 1917, in which the British government expressed support for a "national home for the Jewish people" in Palestine, initiated significant demographic and territorial changes. Jewish organisations began purchasing land from absentee landlords, often displacing Arab tenant farmers in the process. This period set the stage for increasing tensions between Jewish and Arab communities, as the burgeoning Zionist movement sought to establish a Jewish state, leading to conflicts that would escalate in the following decades.

The establishment of the State of Israel in 1948 marked a pivotal moment in Palestinian history, resulting in the Nakba, or "catastrophe," where an estimated 700,000 Palestinians were forcibly displaced from their homes. This mass exodus was not merely a consequence of war; it was part of a broader strategy to secure land for the new state. The Israeli government implemented policies that rendered Palestinians stateless and restricted their rights, including the denial of property claims and the destruction of Palestinian villages. This historical moment fundamentally altered the land ownership landscape and created long-lasting implications for Palestinian identity and rights.

In subsequent decades, the Israeli occupation of the West Bank and Gaza Strip beginning in 1967 further complicated the situation. The establishment of settlements on Palestinian land, often justified under the pretext of security, has been a critical aspect of land displacement strategies. These settlements not only infringe on Palestinian land rights but also disrupt local economies, exacerbate tensions, and contribute to the fragmentation of Palestinian communities. International law, including United Nations resolutions, has consistently affirmed the illegality of these actions, yet enforcement remains elusive, leaving many Palestinians without recourse to justice.

The role of non-governmental organisations (NGOs) has become increasingly vital in advocating for Palestinian land rights amidst this historical backdrop. These organisations work to document land violations, provide legal assistance, and raise awareness about the plight of affected communities. Media representation also plays a crucial role in shaping public perception, often highlighting the resilience of Palestinian communities in the face of adversity. Despite economic hardships and cultural dislocation, many Palestinians continue to assert their rights and maintain their connection to the land, emphasising the importance of historical context in understanding their ongoing struggle for justice and recognition.

Overview of international law relevant to land rights

INTERNATIONAL LAW PLAYS a crucial role in shaping the discourse surrounding land rights, particularly in contexts of conflict and displacement. The principles governing land rights are enshrined in various international treaties, customary laws, and judicial decisions. These legal frameworks establish the rights of individuals and communities to their land, emphasising the importance of protecting property rights and preventing unjust appropriation. Key legal instruments include the Universal Declaration of Human Rights, which affirms the right to property, and the International Covenant on Economic, Social and Cultural Rights, which highlights the need for states to respect and protect the rights of communities to their land and resources.

In the case of Palestine, international law provides a framework to address the ongoing violations of land rights. The application of the Fourth Geneva Convention is particularly relevant, as it prohibits the transfer of an occupying power's civilian population into the territory it occupies, and mandates the protection of civilian populations. Furthermore, United Nations resolutions, such as Resolution 242, call for the withdrawal of Israeli forces from occupied territories and emphasise the inadmissibility of acquiring land by force. These legal standards serve as a basis for advocating for the rights of Palestinians affected by land destruction and displacement.

The role of non-governmental organisations (NGOs) is vital in promoting awareness and compliance with international law regarding land rights in Palestine. NGOs engage in advocacy, documentation, and legal support to highlight violations and mobilise international pressure for accountability. They conduct research and publish reports that detail the impact of land destruction on Palestinian communities, thereby contributing to the historical analysis of land displacement. These organisations also work to amplify the voices of affected communities, ensuring their stories are heard in international forums, and they often serve as intermediaries between these communities and global advocacy networks.

Media representation is another critical aspect that influences public perception and understanding of land rights issues in Palestine. The portrayal of land destruction and displacement in news outlets can shape the narratives around the Israeli-Palestinian conflict. Accurate reporting and comprehensive coverage can raise awareness of the complexities and human consequences of land rights violations, while biased or simplistic narratives may perpetuate misunderstandings and hinder effective advocacy. It is essential for media outlets to approach this subject with sensitivity and a commitment to factual representation, considering the historical and cultural significance of the land to the Palestinian people.

The economic consequences of land destruction extend beyond immediate displacement, affecting the livelihoods and cultural heritage of Palestinian communities. Loss of land often leads to diminished agricultural output, reduced access to resources, and increased poverty levels, resulting in long-term socio-economic challenges. The cultural heritage tied to the land is also at risk, as historical sites and traditional practices are disrupted or destroyed.

Community resilience becomes a key focus, as Palestinians continue to respond to land loss through various means, including grassroots organising and international solidarity efforts. Understanding the intersection of international law, community resistance, and economic impact is essential for a comprehensive approach to advocating for Palestinian land rights.

Objectives of the book

The primary objective of this book is to illuminate the complex interplay between international law and the ongoing struggle for Palestinian land rights, particularly in the context of thuggery, which refers to the systematic destruction of Palestinian land. By examining historical precedents and the legal frameworks that govern land rights, this book aims to provide readers with a comprehensive understanding of how international law has been applied, or in many cases, neglected, in relation to Palestinian land disputes. Through this analysis, we will explore the implications of these legal frameworks on the lives of Palestinians, particularly those who have been directly affected by land loss.

Another key objective is to present a historical analysis of land displacement in Palestine. This section will delve into the events that have led to the current state of land rights in the region, tracing back to the early 20th century and the establishment of various political movements. By highlighting significant milestones and shifts in policy, we aim to foster a deeper understanding of how these historical contexts have shaped contemporary issues. The book will also draw upon case studies of specific Palestinian communities that have faced thuggery, illustrating the human impact of land destruction through personal narratives and community experiences.

In addition to historical and legal perspectives, this book will examine the role of non-governmental organisations (NGOs) in advocating for Palestinian land rights. NGOs have been instrumental in raising awareness, providing legal assistance, and mobilising international support for Palestinian communities. By analysing their strategies and successes, as well as the challenges they face, readers will gain insight into the efficacy of grassroots advocacy in the realm of international law. This exploration will underscore the importance of civil society in amplifying the voices of those whose land rights have been compromised.

Media representation of land destruction in Palestinian areas will also be a focal point of this book. The way in which media portrays these issues can significantly influence public perception and policy responses. By investigating various media narratives and their impact on international discourse, we aim to uncover the biases and challenges inherent in representing the Palestinian struggle. This objective will highlight the role of media as both a tool for awareness and, at times, a barrier to understanding the complexities of land rights issues.

Lastly, this book seeks to address the broader implications of land destruction on Palestinian livelihoods, cultural heritage, and community resilience. Economic consequences stemming from land loss are profound, affecting not only individual families but entire communities and their cultural practices. By presenting case studies that illustrate these economic impacts alongside discussions of community responses to land loss, we aim to emphasise the resilience of the Palestinian people. This multifaceted approach will provide readers with a holistic understanding of the consequences of thuggery while advocating for a more just and equitable resolution to the ongoing struggles for land rights in Palestine.

Chapter 9: Thuggery: Destruction of Palestinian land

Thuggery, a term that has emerged in discussions regarding the destruction of Palestinian land, refers to the systematic and often violent processes that result in the displacement of Palestinian communities and the obliteration of their agricultural and cultural landscapes. This term encapsulates a range of practices including land confiscation, demolition of homes, and the erosion of access to vital resources. Understanding thuggery requires a comprehensive examination of its definition as well as the historical context in which it has unfolded, particularly in relation to Palestinian land rights and the broader implications of international law.

Historically, thuggery can be traced back to the early 20th century, coinciding with the rise of nationalist movements and the subsequent establishment of the State of Israel in 1948. The Nakba, or "catastrophe," marked a pivotal moment when hundreds of thousands of Palestinians were forcibly displaced from their homes, leading to a profound transformation of the land ownership landscape. This initial wave of dispossession set a precedent for ongoing practices of land confiscation, often justified by military and legal frameworks that prioritise state security over individual rights. As new settlements expanded, thuggery became a tool for both territorial control and the erasure of Palestinian heritage.

The impact of thuggery on specific Palestinian communities has been documented through numerous case studies, highlighting the varied experiences of those affected. For instance, the residents of villages like Susiya and Ma'in have faced repeated demolition orders, resulting in the loss of homes and agricultural land. These case studies reveal the intricate relationship between local resistance and the overarching legal frameworks that enable thuggery. They illustrate not only the immediate consequences of land loss but also the long-term effects on community cohesion, identity, and the preservation of cultural heritage.

International law plays a crucial role in the discourse surrounding thuggery, particularly regarding the rights of displaced populations and the legal obligations of states under conventions such as the Fourth Geneva Convention. While international legal frameworks exist to protect the rights of individuals and communities, enforcement remains a significant challenge. Non-governmental organisations have emerged as key advocates, working to document cases of thuggery, raise awareness, and lobby for legal accountability. These organisations play a vital role in providing a platform for affected communities, amplifying their voices, and promoting international solidarity in the face of systemic injustices.

The media representation of land destruction in Palestinian areas significantly influences public perception and policy responses. Coverage often highlights the stark realities of thuggery, showcasing the human cost of land displacement and the resilience of Palestinian communities. However, narratives can vary widely, with some media outlets emphasising security concerns over humanitarian considerations. As communities continue to respond to land loss through activism and cultural preservation efforts, the economic consequences of thuggery remain profound. The destruction of agricultural lands not only threatens livelihoods but also undermines local economies, exacerbating poverty and dependence. Understanding thuggery within this multifaceted context is essential for addressing the ongoing struggle for Palestinian land rights and fostering a more just future.

Mechanisms of land destruction in Palestinian territories

MECHANISMS OF LAND destruction in the Palestinian territories tend to involving a combination of political, legal, and economic factors that systematically undermine the rights of Palestinian communities. One of the primary mechanisms is the expansion of Israeli settlements, which are often established on land that is deemed by international law to belong to Palestinians. These settlements not only lead to direct confiscation of land but also result in the fragmentation of Palestinian territories, making it increasingly difficult for communities to maintain their agricultural practices and livelihoods. The settlements are often accompanied by infrastructure development that further encroaches on Palestinian land, including roads that connect settlements while isolating Palestinian communities.

Another significant mechanism is the use of military orders and regulations that facilitate land confiscation under the pretext of security. The Israeli military frequently issues orders that restrict Palestinian access to their land, claiming security concerns as justification. These regulations can include declaring areas as military zones, which leads to the immediate removal of Palestinian families and the destruction of their homes and farms. Over time, these practices have resulted in the loss of vast tracts of land and have led to a state of uncertainty for many Palestinian farmers, who find themselves unable to cultivate their fields or maintain their traditional lifestyles.

The economic implications of land destruction are profound and have a cascading effect on Palestinian livelihoods. The loss of agricultural land not only diminishes food security but also affects the broader economy by reducing employment opportunities within rural communities. As families are displaced and their lands confiscated, they are often forced into urban areas where job opportunities are scarce and competition is high. This economic displacement exacerbates poverty and leads to a cycle of dependency on international aid, undermining the community's ability to thrive independently.

Culturally, the destruction of land is also an assault on Palestinian identity and heritage. Many Palestinian communities have deep historical ties to their land, which is interwoven with their cultural practices and communal life. The loss of land not only displaces families physically but also erodes their cultural narratives and connections to their ancestors. Cultural heritage sites, often located on the land, face destruction or neglect, further contributing to the loss of identity for future generations. This cultural dimension of land loss is rarely acknowledged in mainstream discussions but is crucial for understanding the broader implications of land destruction.

International law offers frameworks for the protection of land rights, yet enforcement remains a significant challenge. Various resolutions from the United Nations affirm the illegality of settlement expansion and land confiscation, but compliance is often lacking due to political considerations. Non-governmental organisations play a pivotal role in advocating for

Palestinian land rights, documenting violations, and raising awareness about the plight of affected communities. Through advocacy and community engagement, these organisations strive to bring attention to the mechanisms of land destruction and the need for justice for Palestinian land rights, fostering resilience among those impacted and seeking to reclaim their rights under international law.

Impact on Palestinian communities

THE SYSTEMATIC APPROPRIATION and destruction of land have resulted in significant demographic shifts, displacing families and eroding the social fabric of communities. Historical analysis reveals that since the mid-20th century, numerous villages and towns have been forcibly depopulated, leaving behind a legacy of loss and trauma. This displacement not only disrupts lives but also undermines the cultural identity tied to the land, as ancestral homes and communal spaces are obliterated or repurposed.

Case studies of specific Palestinian communities illustrate the direct consequences of thuggery. For instance, the village of Lifta, once a vibrant community near Jerusalem, has faced extensive destruction and neglect since the 1948 Nakba. The remnants of homes and infrastructure serve as a stark reminder of the community that existed, yet these remnants are often left to decay, symbolising the ongoing erasure of Palestinian history. Similarly, in the West Bank, the demolition of homes in areas like East Jerusalem and Area C continues to displace families, forcing them into precarious living conditions while simultaneously expanding Israeli settlements.

International law and land rights in Palestine present a complex legal landscape where violations occur with relative impunity. The Fourth Geneva Convention prohibits the transfer of an occupying power's civilian population into occupied territory and mandates the protection of civilian property. However, enforcement remains inconsistent, leaving Palestinian communities vulnerable to ongoing violations. Advocacy from international organisations highlights these discrepancies, yet the effectiveness of such efforts is often limited by geopolitical realities that complicate intervention.

Non-governmental organisations (NGOs) play a crucial role in advocating for Palestinian land rights and raising awareness about the impact of thuggery.

Through documentation, legal assistance, and community support initiatives, NGOs strive to empower affected communities and highlight their plight on international platforms. These organizations often collaborate with local leaders to ensure that the voices of those impacted are heard, fostering a sense of solidarity and resilience among Palestinians facing land loss.

The economic consequences of land destruction on Palestinian livelihoods are dire, as many families rely on agriculture and local resources for their sustenance. The loss of arable land not only threatens food security but also exacerbates poverty levels within Palestinian communities. Furthermore, the cultural heritage associated with the land, including traditional farming practices and communal gatherings, is at risk of being lost forever. As communities grapple with these challenges, their resilience is manifested in various forms, from grassroots activism to the preservation of cultural narratives, ensuring that their connection to the land endures despite the pervasive threat of erasure.

Chapter 10: Historical analysis of land displacement in Palestine

Key historical events leading to land displacement in Palestine are pivotal in understanding the ongoing struggle for land rights. The 1917 Balfour Declaration marked a significant turning point, as it expressed British support for the establishment of a "national home for the Jewish people" in Palestine, without consulting the indigenous Arab population. This declaration set the stage for increased Jewish immigration to Palestine, which intensified land purchases and transformed demographic dynamics. The following decades saw rising tensions, culminating in the 1947 United Nations partition plan, which proposed dividing Palestine into separate Jewish and Arab states. This plan was met with resistance from the Arab population, leading to widespread violence and the eventual 1948 Arab-Israeli War.

The aftermath of the 1948 conflict resulted in the establishment of the State of Israel and the mass displacement of Palestinians, an event referred to as the Nakba, or "catastrophe." Approximately 700,000 Palestinians were expelled or fled from their homes, with many taking refuge in neighbouring countries or within the newly designated borders of Israel. The destruction of Palestinian villages and the appropriation of land during this period laid the groundwork for ongoing dispossession and the legal complexities surrounding land rights. Many Palestinians find themselves in a state of limbo, unable to return to their ancestral lands, which have been repurposed or repopulated.

The 1967 Six-Day War further exacerbated the situation, as Israel occupied the West Bank and Gaza Strip, along with other territories. This occupation introduced a regime of military rule characterised by land expropriation and settlement expansion. The Israeli government implemented policies aimed at consolidating control over these territories, often justifying land confiscation through security concerns. This period saw the establishment of numerous

Israeli settlements, which not only displaced local Palestinian communities but also created a complicated legal landscape regarding land ownership and rights.

International law, which ostensibly protects the rights of displaced populations, has often been sidelined in the context of Palestinian land rights. Numerous United Nations resolutions have called for the withdrawal of Israeli forces from occupied territories and affirmed the right of return for Palestinian refugees. However, enforcement mechanisms are weak, and the international community's response has been inconsistent. This lack of accountability allows for continued expansion of settlements and ongoing displacement, raising critical questions about justice and the rule of law in relation to Palestinian land rights.

In response to these historical injustices, various non-governmental organisations have emerged, advocating for the protection of Palestinian land and rights. These organisations work to document instances of land destruction, provide legal assistance, and raise awareness of the situation through media representation. Community resilience has also played a crucial role, as affected Palestinian communities have organised protests, legal challenges, and grassroots initiatives to reclaim their rights and preserve their cultural heritage. The economic consequences of land destruction are profound, impacting livelihoods and exacerbating poverty, thereby further complicating the struggle for justice and recognition in the context of Palestinian land rights.

Patterns of displacement in Palestine have evolved through a series of critical historical events that reflect the ongoing struggle for land rights. From the early 20th century, the establishment of the Zionist movement marked the beginning of systematic land acquisition and the subsequent displacement of Palestinian communities. The Balfour Declaration of 1917, which endorsed the establishment of a Jewish homeland in Palestine, set the stage for land dispossession. This initial political manoeuvring facilitated the influx of Jewish immigrants and initiated tensions over land ownership, leading to widespread displacement and the fragmentation of Palestinian communities.

The culmination of these tensions was starkly illustrated during the 1948 Arab-Israeli War, known to Palestinians as the Nakba, or catastrophe. This event resulted in the forced expulsion of over 700,000 Palestinians from their homes and the destruction of hundreds of villages. The demographic changes that ensued were not merely a byproduct of war but a calculated strategy to reshape the land and its population. The establishment of the State of Israel was accompanied by laws that effectively marginalised Palestinian land claims, further entrenching patterns of displacement that would continue to evolve in subsequent decades.

Throughout the latter half of the 20th century, particularly during the 1967 Six-Day War, Israel's occupation of the West Bank and Gaza Strip heralded a new phase of displacement. The expansion of settlements, often deemed illegal under international law, led to the appropriation of vast tracts of Palestinian land. These settlements, coupled with military checkpoints and restrictions on movement, have systematically dismantled the social fabric of Palestinian communities. The impact of these actions has been profound, as families have been uprooted, crops destroyed, and ancestral lands lost, perpetuating a cycle of displacement and dispossession.

The role of international law in addressing these patterns of displacement has been complex and often ineffective. While numerous United Nations resolutions and legal frameworks recognise the rights of displaced populations and the illegality of settlement expansion, enforcement remains a significant challenge. The lack of accountability for violations of international law has allowed the cycle of land destruction to continue unabated. Non-governmental organisations have attempted to fill this gap by documenting human rights abuses, advocating for policy changes, and supporting displaced communities. However, their efforts often face significant obstacles, including political resistance and limited resources.

In response to these ongoing challenges, Palestinian communities have demonstrated remarkable resilience. Grassroots movements have emerged, focusing on land reclamation, cultural preservation, and legal advocacy to counteract the effects of displacement. These initiatives highlight the deep connection between Palestinians and their land, emphasising the importance of cultural heritage in their struggle for justice. The economic consequences of land destruction have also galvanised community efforts, as livelihoods tied to agriculture and local resources are threatened. The ongoing patterns of displacement thus reflect not only a historical narrative of loss but also a contemporary struggle for rights, identity, and dignity in the face of adversity.

Analysis of legal frameworks pre- and post-displacement

THE LEGAL FRAMEWORKS governing land rights in Palestine have evolved significantly before and after the displacement of Palestinian communities. Prior to displacement, the Ottoman land laws and British Mandate regulations established a complex system of land ownership that recognised various forms of tenure, including private ownership, communal rights, and state land. These frameworks provided a legal basis for land claims, yet they were often undermined by broader geopolitical interests. The historical context of land ownership was further complicated by colonial policies that favoured Jewish immigration and land acquisition, paving the way for future conflicts over land rights.

Following the mass displacement of Palestinians in 1948, the legal landscape shifted dramatically. The newly established Israeli state implemented a series of laws that effectively redefined land ownership. The Absentee Property Law allowed the state to seize land from those who had fled or were forcibly removed, while the Land Acquisition Law facilitated the appropriation of land for state purposes. These laws were framed as necessary for national security and development, yet they significantly eroded the legal rights of Palestinian landowners, leading to widespread dispossession and a lack of recourse for those affected.

International law plays a crucial role in analysing the legitimacy of these legal frameworks. The Fourth Geneva Convention prohibits the transfer of an occupying power's civilian population into occupied territory and restricts the appropriation of land for military purposes. However, the application of international law regarding Palestine remains contentious, as enforcement mechanisms are weak and often politicised. The lack of accountability for violations of international law exacerbates the plight of displaced Palestinians, leaving communities vulnerable to ongoing land loss and destruction.

Non-governmental organizations (NGOs) have emerged as vital advocates for Palestinian land rights, seeking to challenge the legal frameworks that facilitate land dispossession. Through documentation, legal aid, and advocacy campaigns, NGOs work to raise awareness of the impact of Israeli policies on Palestinian communities. They engage with international bodies to hold Israel accountable for violations of human rights and to promote the recognition of Palestinian land rights within the global legal framework. This advocacy is critical in amplifying the voices of affected communities and in pushing for legal reforms that align with international standards.

The analysis of legal frameworks pre- and post-displacement reveals a stark contrast in the treatment of land rights in Palestine. While historical laws offered some recognition of Palestinian land ownership, the subsequent legal developments have largely favoured the interests of the Israeli state at the expense of Palestinian communities. Understanding this legal context is essential for comprehending the broader struggle for justice and land rights in Palestine, as it highlights the need for an informed and engaged international community that supports the pursuit of legal remedies and recognises the historical injustices faced by Palestinians.

Chapter 11: Case studies of specific Palestinian communities affected by thuggery

Case Study: The Village of Lifta

The village of Lifta, located on the outskirts of Jerusalem, serves as a poignant case study illustrating the impact of land displacement on Palestinian communities. Once a thriving village known for its natural springs and agricultural lands, Lifta was depopulated during the 1948 Arab-Israeli War. Many of its residents were forcibly removed from their homes, leading to a significant loss of not only their physical properties but also their cultural heritage. The empty structures of Lifta stand as a testament to the village's rich history and the collective memory of its inhabitants, who were denied the right to return.

In the context of international law, Lifta's situation highlights the complexities surrounding land rights and the legal frameworks that govern displacement. The principles laid out in various international treaties, such as the Fourth Geneva Convention, emphasise the protection of civilian populations during armed conflicts and the prohibition of forced displacement. Despite these provisions, the case of Lifta illustrates a gap between international law and its enforcement, as the village remains in a state of neglect and disrepair, serving as a symbol of the broader struggle for justice experienced by Palestinians.

Non-governmental organisations (NGOs) play a crucial role in advocating for the rights of communities like Lifta. Through documentation, legal assistance, and awareness-raising efforts, these organisations aim to shed light on the ongoing violations faced by Palestinians. They work tirelessly to engage the international community, urging them to hold accountable those responsible for land destruction and displacement. The resilience demonstrated by NGOs in preserving the history of Lifta and other affected areas is essential in the fight against the erasure of Palestinian identity and rights.

Media representation of Lifta and similar villages is critical in shaping public perception and understanding of the Palestinian experience. Coverage that highlights the historical context of land loss emphasises the human stories behind the statistics. By portraying the emotional and cultural significance of Lifta, media narratives can foster empathy and support for Palestinian rights. The challenge remains, however, in ensuring that these stories are told authentically and without bias, as misrepresentation can perpetuate misconceptions and hinder efforts for justice.

The economic consequences of land destruction in Lifta resonate deeply within the broader Palestinian community. Displacement has disrupted traditional livelihoods, leading to increased poverty and unemployment rates among former residents and their descendants. The loss of agricultural land not only impacts food security but also erodes the cultural practices tied to land stewardship. Despite these challenges, the resilience of the people from Lifta manifests in their ongoing efforts to reclaim their narrative, preserve their heritage, and advocate for their rights on both local and international platforms.

The Bedouin communities in the Negev

THE BEDOUIN COMMUNITIES in the Negev offer a poignant case study of the broader struggles faced by Palestinian communities regarding land rights and displacement. Historically, these communities have inhabited the Negev desert for generations, developing a unique cultural identity deeply intertwined with their land. However, the establishment of the State of Israel and subsequent policies aimed at land consolidation and urban development have led to significant challenges for the Bedouins. These policies often manifest in the form of home demolitions, restrictions on movement, and the denial of basic services, all of which threaten their traditional way of life and cultural heritage.

One of the critical aspects of the Bedouin experience is the ongoing issue of land dispossession. The Israeli government has classified much of the land traditionally used by Bedouin communities as state land or has allocated it for development projects, which has led to the forced relocation of these communities. International law recognises the rights of indigenous peoples to their ancestral lands, yet the Bedouins have found their claims largely disregarded by state authorities. This situation highlights a significant gap between international legal standards and their application on the ground, raising questions about the effectiveness of these laws in protecting vulnerable populations like the Bedouins.

The role of non-governmental organisations (NGOs) has been crucial in advocating for the rights of Bedouin communities in the Negev. Various NGOs have documented human rights abuses, provided legal assistance, and raised awareness about the plight of the Bedouins both locally and internationally. These organisations serve not only as advocates but also as vital support systems, helping the communities navigate the complexities of land rights and legal battles. Their efforts underscore the importance of civil society in holding governments accountable and promoting justice for marginalised groups.

Media representation plays a significant role in shaping public perception of the Bedouin communities and their struggles. Coverage of the Bedouins often focuses on dramatic events such as home demolitions or protests, which can sometimes overshadow the day-to-day realities faced by these communities. A more nuanced portrayal that includes the cultural richness and resilience of the Bedouin people is essential for fostering a broader understanding of their plight. Such representation can also galvanise public support for their cause and encourage solidarity movements that advocate for justice and land rights.

Ultimately, the resilience of Bedouin communities in the Negev is a testament to their enduring connection to their land and culture. Despite facing systemic challenges, these communities continue to assert their rights and adapt to changing circumstances. Their experiences reflect a broader narrative of struggle and resistance among Palestinian communities affected by land destruction. Recognising the significance of their plight not only sheds light on the injustices they face but also emphasises the need for a concerted effort to uphold international law and advocate for the rights of all Palestinians in their struggle for land and dignity.

Case study: The Impact on Gaza Strip communities

The Gaza Strip has long been a focal point of conflict and humanitarian crisis, with communities facing severe challenges due to ongoing land destruction and displacement. This case study examines the impact of these dynamics on the residents of Gaza, highlighting how the systematic destruction of land has not only disrupted livelihoods but also eroded the cultural and historical fabric of the communities. The unique geographic and political circumstances of the Gaza Strip exacerbate the vulnerabilities faced by its inhabitants, making it a critical area for understanding the broader implications of land rights violations in Palestine.

One of the most immediate effects of land destruction in Gaza is the significant economic decline experienced by local communities. The blockade and military operations have severely restricted access to vital resources, such as water, agricultural land, and infrastructure. Farmers have seen their lands destroyed or rendered unusable, which has led to a decline in agricultural production, a cornerstone of the Gazan economy. The loss of arable land not only impacts food security but also exacerbates poverty, as many families rely on agriculture for their livelihoods. This economic disenfranchisement is compounded by the lack of employment opportunities in other sectors, leading to a cycle of dependency and hardship.

The cultural heritage of Gaza's communities is equally at risk due to land destruction. Historical sites, traditional farming practices, and community spaces that have been integral to Gazan identity are disappearing. The erasure of these elements contributes to a loss of collective memory and cultural continuity, leaving younger generations disconnected from their heritage. This cultural dislocation can have profound psychological effects on the community, as individuals grapple with a sense of loss and displacement that transcends mere physical land.

Community resilience emerges as a critical theme in the face of these challenges. Gazans have demonstrated remarkable strength and adaptability, finding ways to cope with the ongoing loss of land and resources. Initiatives aimed at community rebuilding, cultural preservation, and economic diversification are essential for fostering resilience. Grassroots movements, local cooperatives, and cultural programs serve not only as mechanisms for survival but also as expressions of resistance against the narrative of erasure. Ultimately, the impact of land destruction on Gaza Strip communities extends beyond immediate economic and cultural losses; it challenges the very essence of identity and existence for its people.

Chapter 12: International law and land rights in Palestine

International Humanitarian Law (IHL) is a set of rules that seek to limit the effects of armed conflict for humanitarian reasons. It aims to protect persons who are not participating in hostilities and to regulate the means and methods of warfare. IHL is grounded in principles of humanity, neutrality, and impartiality, and it is crucial for understanding the legal frameworks applicable to situations of conflict, such as those experienced in Palestine. The Geneva Conventions and their Additional Protocols are central components of IHL, outlining the obligations of states and non-state actors during armed conflicts, including the treatment of civilians and the protection of property.

In the context of Palestine, the application of IHL becomes particularly significant given the prolonged nature of the conflict and the ongoing issues of land displacement and destruction. The unlawful seizure of land, destruction of property, and forced displacement of civilians are often cited as violations of IHL. The principles of distinction and proportionality under IHL are meant to ensure that military operations do not indiscriminately harm civilians or civilian infrastructure, yet evidence suggests that these principles have frequently been overlooked in the region, exacerbating the plight of Palestinian communities.

Furthermore, the role of state parties in upholding IHL is critical. States are obligated to ensure respect for these laws and to take action against violations. However, the international community's response to violations of IHL in Palestine has often been criticised as insufficient. The lack of accountability for those responsible for violations, combined with political complexities, leads to a situation where the rights of Palestinians, particularly regarding their land and property, are frequently undermined. This raises questions about the efficacy of IHL in protecting vulnerable populations and the need for stronger enforcement mechanisms.

Non-Governmental Organizations (NGOs) play a vital role in advocating for Palestinian land rights within the framework of IHL. These organisations often document violations, provide legal assistance, and raise awareness about the impact of land destruction on Palestinian communities. By leveraging international legal standards, NGOs seek to hold violators accountable and promote the rights of affected populations. Their efforts are essential in bringing to light the realities on the ground, which can sometimes be obscured by political narratives and media representation.

Community resilience in the face of land loss is another important aspect of the IHL discourse. Palestinian communities have demonstrated remarkable strength and resourcefulness in responding to the challenges posed by land destruction and displacement. Their strategies often include legal battles, advocacy for rights, and the preservation of cultural heritage, all of which are informed by an understanding of their rights under international law. The interplay between IHL and community resilience highlights the importance of both legal frameworks and grassroots efforts in the ongoing struggle for justice and recognition of Palestinian land rights.

The United Nations has issued a series of resolutions addressing the Israeli-Palestinian conflict, particularly focusing on issues related to land rights and territorial disputes. These resolutions, although non-binding, carry significant weight in international discourse and serve as a framework for understanding the international community's stance on the conflict. Resolution 242, passed in 1967, called for the withdrawal of Israeli armed forces from territories occupied during the Six-Day War and emphasised the necessity of achieving a just settlement of the refugee problem. This resolution, among others, has been pivotal in framing discussions around Palestinian land rights and the legitimacy of claims made by both sides.

The implications of these resolutions extend beyond mere political statements; they influence legal precedents and international norms regarding land sovereignty and human rights. For Palestinians, the UN resolutions provide a reference point for legal claims to land ownership and the right to self-determination. However, the effectiveness of these resolutions has often been undermined by the lack of enforcement mechanisms. Countries and international bodies may express support for these resolutions, but without a robust means of implementation, the resolutions can turn into symbolic gestures rather than tools for tangible change.

Moreover, the responses to these resolutions from various actors shape the landscape of Palestinian land rights. Israel's consistent rejection of specific resolutions, particularly those calling for a halt to settlement expansion, highlights the challenges of achieving compliance with international law. This defiance has led to an ongoing cycle of land dispossession and destruction, often referred to as "thuggery." This term encapsulates the violent and coercive methods employed to displace Palestinian communities, exacerbating the historical narrative of land loss that continues to affect generations.

Non-governmental organisations play a critical role in advocating for the implementation of UN resolutions and raising awareness about the plight of affected Palestinian communities. These organisations often document cases of land destruction and displacement, providing valuable data that support the legal arguments for Palestinian land rights. Their efforts help to mobilise international public opinion and engage with global advocacy networks, emphasising the need for accountability and adherence to international law. Through various campaigns and reports, these NGOs highlight the human and cultural costs of land loss, contributing to a broader understanding of the issue.

The media's representation of these resolutions and the ongoing situation in Palestinian territories also significantly influences public perception and policy-making. Coverage of the destruction of Palestinian land often reflects broader narratives around justice, human rights, and international law. As such, the media can serve as a double-edged sword, either reinforcing dominant narratives that downplay Palestinian rights or amplifying calls for justice and accountability. Understanding the implications of UN resolutions within this context reveals the complexities of the struggle for Palestinian land rights and the multifaceted responses required to address the ongoing injustices faced by Palestinian communities.

Challenges in enforcing land rights

THE ENFORCEMENT OF land rights in Palestine faces numerous challenges that complicate the pursuit of justice for displaced communities.

One significant barrier is the complex legal framework that governs land ownership and usage, which is often influenced by various historical events, including the establishment of the State of Israel in 1948 and subsequent military occupations. This framework is characterised by a mix of Ottoman, British Mandate, Jordanian, and Israeli laws, making it difficult for Palestinian landowners to navigate their rights effectively. The fragmented nature of these laws often results in confusion and a lack of clear legal recourse for Palestinians seeking to reclaim their land.

Another challenge arises from the political dynamics surrounding land rights enforcement. The Israeli government's policies and practices, including settlement expansion and land confiscation, have created a hostile environment for Palestinians. These actions are often justified under the guise of security or development, yet they undermine the legal claims of Palestinians to their ancestral lands. The power imbalance between the Israeli state and Palestinian communities further exacerbates the difficulties in asserting land rights, as the latter often lack the resources and political support necessary to challenge such policies effectively.

Additionally, the role of international law in protecting land rights presents its own set of challenges. While international legal frameworks, such as the Fourth Geneva Convention, provide guidelines for the protection of occupied territories and the rights of displaced persons, enforcement mechanisms remain weak. The international community's response to violations of these laws is often inconsistent, with geopolitical interests influencing the degree of accountability imposed on Israel. This lack of effective enforcement diminishes the prospects for justice, leading many Palestinians to feel disillusioned with the system meant to protect their rights.

Non-governmental organisations (NGOs) play a crucial role in advocating for Palestinian land rights, yet they also encounter significant obstacles. Funding restrictions, political pressures, and the challenging operational environment in the occupied territories hinder their ability to effectively address land issues. Many NGOs are tasked with documenting violations, providing legal assistance, and raising awareness about land rights, but their efforts are often met with resistance from Israeli authorities. This creates a precarious situation where the advocacy work of these organizations can be stifled, limiting their impact on the ground.

Lastly, the cultural implications of land loss is deplorable for many Palestinians, land is not merely a physical space but embodies their history, identity, and connection to their heritage. The destruction and displacement resulting from thuggery—an Arabic term for the systematic destruction of Palestinian land—have profound emotional and psychological effects on communities. As they navigate these challenges, Palestinians continue to demonstrate resilience through various forms of resistance, from peaceful protests to legal battles, illustrating their enduring connection to the land and their unwavering commitment to asserting their rights.

Chapter 13: The role of non-Governmental organisations in advocating for Palestinian land

Non-governmental organisations (NGOs) play a critical role in advocating for Palestinian land rights, focusing their efforts on both immediate humanitarian needs and long-term systemic change. Prominent NGOs such as B'Tselem, Al-Haq, and the Palestinian Centre for Human Rights have established missions that address the multifaceted challenges faced by Palestinian communities. These organizations aim to document human rights violations, provide legal assistance, and raise awareness about the ongoing impacts of land displacement and destruction. Their work is rooted in international law, seeking to hold both local and international actors accountable for injustices against Palestinians.

B'Tselem, an Israeli human rights organisation, is dedicated to documenting human rights violations in the occupied territories. Its mission emphasises the importance of transparency and accountability, providing detailed reports and analysis on issues such as land confiscation, home demolitions, and settler violence. By gathering testimonies from affected individuals and publishing findings, B'Tselem not only highlights the plight of Palestinians but also seeks to influence public opinion and policy within Israel and the international community. Their advocacy work is aimed at ensuring that the voices of those affected by land destruction are heard and recognised.

Al-Haq, a Palestinian NGO, focuses on promoting and protecting human rights and the rule of law in the West Bank and Gaza Strip. Its mission includes legal advocacy, documentation of violations, and engaging with international bodies to hold Israel accountable for its actions. Al-Haq's work extends to providing legal aid to individuals facing displacement and advocating for policy changes that respect Palestinian land rights. By utilising international legal frameworks, Al-Haq seeks to empower Palestinian communities and strengthen their claims to land and resources while raising awareness of the broader implications of occupation.

The Palestinian Centre for Human Rights (PCHR) emphasises the importance of legal advocacy and community support in its mission. PCHR provides legal assistance to victims of human rights violations, often focusing on cases involving land rights and access to resources. Their work not only addresses immediate legal needs but also aims to build resilience within communities affected by land loss. By offering education and resources, PCHR empowers individuals to advocate for their rights and engage in the political process, thereby fostering a sense of agency in the face of systemic challenges.

These NGOs, among others, serve as critical actors in the struggle for Palestinian land rights. Through their missions, they aim to confront the injustices of land destruction and displacement, advocating for accountability and fostering resilience within Palestinian communities. Their combined efforts highlight the importance of international law in addressing the complexities of the Palestinian situation, while also underscoring the need for a coordinated response to the ongoing threat of land loss. By raising awareness and advocating for change, these organisations contribute significantly to the broader discourse on justice and rights in Palestine.

Strategies employed by NGOs for advocacy

NON-GOVERNMENTAL ORGANISATIONS (NGOs) play a crucial role in advocating for Palestinian land rights, employing a variety of strategies to draw attention to the injustices faced by Palestinian communities. One primary strategy is the use of documentation and research to provide evidence of land displacement and destruction. NGOs systematically collect data on land confiscations, the impact of military operations, and settlement expansions. This information is often compiled into reports that highlight the extent of the violations, making it accessible to policymakers, media, and the public. By grounding their advocacy in empirical evidence, NGOs strengthen their arguments and enhance their credibility in the international arena.

Advocacy campaigns are another key strategy utilised by NGOs to raise awareness about Palestinian land rights. These campaigns often leverage social media, traditional media outlets, and public events to disseminate their messages widely. Through storytelling and visual imagery, NGOs aim to humanise the statistics and reports they produce, illustrating the lived experiences of those affected by land loss. This approach not only engages the public but also fosters a sense of solidarity and urgency around the issue. Collaborative campaigns with other organisations, both local and international, further amplify their reach and impact, creating a united front against land injustices.

Legal advocacy is also a significant strategy employed by NGOs to challenge unlawful practices related to land rights. Many organisations work with international legal experts to navigate the complexities of international law, seeking to hold violators accountable. This may involve filing complaints with international bodies, engaging in litigation, or supporting local communities in their legal battles. By framing land rights issues within the context of international legal frameworks, NGOs aim to increase pressure on states and corporations complicit in land dispossession. This legal approach not only seeks immediate redress but also aims to establish precedents that can protect Palestinian land rights in the long term.

Education and capacity building within Palestinian communities represent another vital strategy. NGOs often conduct workshops and training sessions to empower local populations with knowledge about their rights and the tools available to defend them. This grassroots approach fosters resilience and encourages community mobilisation. By equipping individuals with the skills to advocate for themselves, NGOs help to cultivate a sense of agency and collective action among affected communities. This empowerment is essential in the face of ongoing challenges, as it enables communities to articulate their narratives and assert their rights in various forums.

Finally, NGOs engage in coalition-building with a diverse array of stakeholders, including other NGOs, academic institutions, and grassroots movements. These coalitions enhance the effectiveness of advocacy efforts by pooling resources, sharing knowledge, and coordinating actions. Such collaborations can lead to more comprehensive strategies that address the multifaceted nature of land rights issues. By creating a network of support that spans different sectors and geographies, NGOs can amplify their advocacy and increase the likelihood of achieving meaningful change. This collective approach not only addresses immediate concerns but also seeks long-term solutions to the systemic injustices faced by Palestinian communities.

Case Examples of successful advocacy campaigns

CASE EXAMPLES OF SUCCESSFUL advocacy campaigns illustrate the power of collective action and strategic communication in the fight for Palestinian land rights. One notable example is the campaign led by the Palestinian NGO Al-Haq, which focused on raising awareness about land confiscation and its impact on local communities. Through meticulous documentation of land dispossession and human rights violations, Al-Haq successfully engaged international legal bodies and human rights organisations. Their efforts culminated in a comprehensive report that was presented to the United Nations, which helped to draw global attention to the issue and pressure governments to reconsider their stances on Israeli settlement policies.

Another significant campaign was orchestrated by the grassroots organisation Stop the Wall, which mobilised Palestinian communities to resist the construction of the separation barrier in the West Bank. By organising peaceful protests and leveraging social media platforms, Stop the Wall highlighted the adverse effects of the barrier on Palestinian lives and land. Their advocacy led to increased international solidarity, with prominent figures and activists joining their cause. This campaign not only raised awareness but also influenced public opinion and policy discussions in various countries, leading to calls for accountability regarding the impact of the barrier on Palestinian territories.

The Boycott, Divestment, Sanctions (BDS) movement represents a successful example of a global advocacy campaign aimed at ending Israeli occupation and promoting Palestinian rights. Initiated in 2005 by a coalition of Palestinian civil society organisations, the BDS movement has gained traction through strategic campaigns that highlight the connection between consumer behaviour and the ongoing injustices faced by Palestinians. By encouraging individuals and institutions worldwide to boycott Israeli products and divest from companies supporting the occupation, the movement has successfully influenced economic and political discourse, prompting some governments and organisations to take a stand against Israeli policies.

The role of international NGOs such as Human Rights Watch and Amnesty International has also been crucial in advancing the cause of Palestinian land rights. These organisations have conducted extensive research and published reports that document violations of international law, including the illegal annexation of Palestinian land. Their findings have not only raised awareness but have also served as a basis for legal action in various jurisdictions. These reports have empowered local communities and activists by providing them with the evidence needed to advocate for their rights both locally and internationally.

Lastly, the success of media campaigns, particularly during periods of heightened conflict, has played a pivotal role in shaping the narrative around Palestinian land rights. During the 2014 Gaza conflict, social media platforms became instrumental in disseminating real-time information about the destruction of Palestinian homes and infrastructure. Activists used hashtags and viral content to engage a global audience, prompting widespread discussions about the humanitarian consequences of military actions. This visibility has pressured international actors to respond and has fostered a greater understanding of the complexities surrounding land rights issues in Palestine. These case examples underscore the effectiveness of advocacy campaigns in challenging injustices and mobilising support for Palestinian communities facing land dispossession.

Chapter 14: Media representation of land destruction in Palestinian areas

The media coverage of Palestinian land rights and the phenomenon of thuggery has evolved significantly over the decades, reflecting shifts in geopolitical dynamics, public sentiment, and technological advancements. Initially, mainstream media tended to portray the Israeli-Palestinian conflict through a simplistic lens, often favouring narratives that aligned with powerful state interests. This resulted in a lack of nuanced understanding of the complexities surrounding land displacement and destruction. Early reports frequently highlighted violent confrontations without adequately addressing the underlying issues of land rights and historical grievances, which contributed to a misrepresentation of Palestinian experiences and struggles.

As the conflict progressed, particularly following pivotal events such as the First and Second Intifadas, media coverage began to shift. Journalists and media outlets started to recognize the importance of local voices and grassroots movements. This change was partly driven by the emergence of new media platforms, allowing Palestinians to document their experiences and share their stories directly with a global audience. The rise of social media provided a powerful tool for advocacy, enabling communities to present firsthand accounts of the impacts of thuggery and land loss. As a result, reporting became more multifaceted, incorporating personal narratives that highlighted the human cost of land destruction.

Despite these advancements, media representation of Palestinian land rights remains inconsistent. While some outlets provide in-depth coverage of specific incidents of thuggery, others revert to framing the issue within a binary conflict narrative. This can lead to the minimisation of the historical context surrounding land displacement and the systematic nature of the destruction faced by Palestinian communities. Additionally, the influence of political agendas often shapes media narratives, which can skew public perception and hinder comprehensive understanding. The challenge remains for media professionals to move beyond surface-level reporting and engage with the broader implications of land rights within international law.

The role of non-governmental organisations (NGOs) in advocating for Palestinian land rights has also been pivotal in shaping media narratives. NGOs often serve as vital sources of information and research, providing data and analysis that can inform journalists and enhance public discourse. Their advocacy efforts raise awareness about the legal frameworks governing land rights, and they frequently collaborate with media outlets to highlight specific case studies of affected communities. Through these partnerships, NGOs have facilitated deeper investigations into the economic and cultural consequences of land destruction, thereby enriching the media landscape with critical insights.

In recent years, there has been a growing recognition of the resilience of Palestinian communities in the face of land loss. Media coverage increasingly acknowledges these communities' efforts to resist displacement and assert their rights. This shift not only empowers Palestinian voices but also emphasizes the importance of cultural heritage in the struggle for land rights. By focusing on community responses to thuggery and the economic ramifications of land destruction, the media can help foster a more comprehensive understanding of the ongoing struggle for justice and rights in Palestine. This evolving narrative has the potential to influence public opinion and inspire greater advocacy for meaningful change within the realm of international law and human rights.

The role of social media in shaping public perception

THE ADVENT OF SOCIAL media has transformed the way information is disseminated and consumed, playing a crucial role in shaping public perception regarding complex issues, including the struggle for Palestinian land rights. Platforms such as Twitter, Facebook, and Instagram enable real-time sharing of events, opinions, and personal stories from individuals directly affected by land displacement. This immediacy allows for a more nuanced understanding of the realities on the ground, challenging mainstream narratives that may overlook or simplify the Palestinian experience. By amplifying voices that have long been marginalised, social media serves as a powerful tool for advocacy and awareness.

In the context of Palestinian land rights, social media facilitates the documentation and dissemination of information related to thuggery, or the systematic destruction of Palestinian land. Activists use these platforms to share firsthand accounts, images, and videos that capture the impact of land loss on communities. By highlighting specific cases, such as the destruction of homes and agricultural lands, social media can evoke empathy and motivate action among global audiences. This grassroots storytelling contrasts sharply with traditional media, which may present a more sanitised or detached view of the conflict, often failing to convey the human cost associated with land dispossession.

Moreover, social media has become an essential arena for mobilising support for non-governmental organisations that advocate for Palestinian land rights. These organisations utilise social media to inform followers about their initiatives, share reports on land rights violations, and promote campaigns aimed at raising awareness and funds. The interactive nature of social media allows for dynamic engagement between organisations and their supporters, fostering a sense of community that transcends geographical boundaries. This engagement can lead to increased international pressure on governments and institutions to address the injustices faced by Palestinians.

The media representation of land destruction in Palestinian areas has also been significantly influenced by social media. Traditional media outlets often rely on established narratives that may not capture the complexity of the situation. In contrast, social media allows for a multiplicity of voices and perspectives, enabling users to curate their narratives around land loss and resistance. This decentralisation of information can challenge dominant media portrayals that perpetuate stereotypes or ignore the historical context of displacement. As a result, social media plays a critical role in reshaping narratives that inform public perception and policy discussions.

Lastly, the resilience demonstrated by Palestinian communities in response to land loss is often highlighted on social media, showcasing their resistance and efforts to reclaim their rights. Posts about community initiatives, cultural heritage preservation, and economic alternatives reflect a determination to maintain identity and dignity despite ongoing challenges. By sharing these stories, social media not only raises awareness of the struggles faced but also celebrates the strength and agency of Palestinian communities. This representation is vital in fostering a more comprehensive understanding of the socio-economic and cultural ramifications of land destruction, encouraging solidarity and support from a global audience.

Case studies of prominent media narratives

CASE STUDIES OF PROMINENT media narratives surrounding the struggle for Palestinian land rights reveal the complex interplay between reporting, public perception, and the realities on the ground. One significant case is the portrayal of the land confiscation in the village of Bil'in, where residents engaged in weekly protests against the construction of the Israeli separation barrier. Media coverage highlighted the resilience of the community and the impact of international solidarity movements, illustrating how local resistance can capture global attention. The consistent narrative of peaceful protest juxtaposed with violent repression served to humanise the struggle and underscore the broader implications of land loss for Palestinian identity.

Another important narrative emerged from the destruction of olive groves in the West Bank. Olive trees symbolise Palestinian heritage and economic stability, making their destruction a poignant representation of land confiscation. Media reports often featured personal stories of farmers who lost their livelihoods, emphasising the economic consequences of land destruction. This narrative not only showcased the immediate impact on local communities but also sparked discussions about cultural heritage and the role of agriculture in Palestinian society, highlighting the intricate connections between land, identity, and resistance.

The case of Sheikh Jarrah in East Jerusalem further exemplifies how media narratives shape public understanding of land rights issues. The ongoing evictions of Palestinian families from their homes have garnered international media attention, transforming a local struggle into a global cause. Coverage has focused on the legal battles faced by residents, the historical context of the neighbourhood, and the broader implications of displacement. The framing of these evictions as a violation of international law resonates with global audiences, prompting widespread advocacy and calls for action from various non-governmental organisations.

Media narratives also reflect the complexities of international law and its application to the Israeli-Palestinian conflict. Reports on land rights often reference United Nations resolutions and legal frameworks that support Palestinian claims. However, the interpretation of these laws can be contentious, with differing perspectives influencing public discourse. By examining these narratives, one can understand how media representations can either reinforce or challenge existing power dynamics, shaping perceptions of legitimacy and justice in the context of land rights.

The role of non-governmental organisations in advocating for Palestinian land rights is another critical aspect of these media narratives. Organisations like B'Tselem and the Palestinian Centre for Human Rights effectively utilise media platforms to raise awareness about land destruction and displacement. Their reports and campaigns often provide the necessary context and statistics to support the personal stories highlighted in mainstream media. This collaboration enhances the visibility of Palestinian struggles and emphasises the importance of community resilience in the face of ongoing challenges, ultimately contributing to a more nuanced understanding of the broader implications of land loss in Palestine.

Chapter 15: Community resilience: Palestinian responses to land loss

Grassroots movements have emerged as a significant force in the struggle for Palestinian land rights, mobilising communities at the local, national, and international levels to advocate for justice and recognition. These movements often arise in response to the systematic destruction of Palestinian land, 'thuggery', which has deeply affected the social, economic, and cultural fabric of Palestinian communities. Through organised efforts, grassroots movements not only raise awareness about land displacement but also foster a sense of solidarity and resilience among affected populations, empowering them to advocate for their rights and reclaim their narratives.

One of the key impacts of grassroots movements is their ability to document and highlight the historical injustices faced by Palestinians. By collecting testimonies, conducting research, and disseminating information, these movements provide a counter-narrative to dominant discourses that often ignore or downplay the extent of land displacement. They engage in historical analysis, examining the policies and practices that have led to the loss of Palestinian land over decades. This historical context is vital for understanding current struggles, as it connects past injustices to ongoing violations of international law and human rights.

Grassroots movements also play a critical role in facilitating case studies of specific Palestinian communities affected by thuggery. By focusing on individual stories, from villages facing demolition to families displaced from their ancestral homes, these movements personalise the broader struggle for land rights. Such case studies serve to humanise the statistics often cited in international discussions, bringing attention to the lived experiences of those impacted by land loss. This approach not only educates the public but also engages policymakers and advocates to consider the unique challenges faced by different communities when formulating responses to land rights issues.

The role of non-governmental organisations (NGOs) in supporting grassroots movements cannot be overstated. Many NGOs provide crucial resources, training, and platforms for grassroots activists to amplify their messages. They assist in legal advocacy, help to navigate the complexities of international law regarding land rights, and promote campaigns that draw international attention to the plight of Palestinian communities. Together, grassroots movements and NGOs create a robust network that enhances advocacy efforts, making them more effective in lobbying for policy changes and raising awareness on global platforms.

Media representation of land destruction in Palestinian areas significantly influences public perception and awareness. Grassroots movements often engage with media outlets to ensure that stories of land loss and community resilience reach wider audiences. They utilise social media and traditional journalism to document and disseminate real-time accounts of land dispossession and resistance. This media engagement not only helps to raise international consciousness about the plight of Palestinians but also fosters a sense of global solidarity with grassroots campaigns, ultimately contributing to a more informed and active international community advocating for justice and land rights in Palestine.

Cultural practices and land stewardship

CULTURAL PRACTICES among Palestinian communities are deeply intertwined with their land, shaping identities, traditions, and social structures. The concept of land stewardship in Palestine transcends mere agricultural practices; it embodies a holistic relationship with the environment, where the land is seen as a vital source of cultural heritage and communal memory. Traditional agricultural methods, such as terracing and the cultivation of indigenous crops, reflect not only a sustainable approach to land use but also a profound respect for the ancestral connection to the land. This relationship has been threatened by ongoing land displacement, which disrupts these practices and erodes the cultural identity tied to specific geographies.

The historical context of land displacement in Palestine reveals a systematic pattern of land appropriation and cultural erasure. Various waves of colonisation and conflict have resulted in the fragmentation of Palestinian communities and the disruption of their traditional land management practices. This transformation has often been accompanied by the imposition of foreign agricultural methods that disregard local knowledge and customs. The loss of land has not only economic implications but also cultural ramifications, as communities find it increasingly difficult to pass down traditional agricultural practices and the associated knowledge to future generations.

Case studies highlighting specific Palestinian communities affected by land destruction provide critical insights into the resilience of these communities in the face of adversity. For instance, in areas like the Jordan Valley and the villages facing the encroachment of settlements, local populations have developed innovative strategies to reclaim their narratives and assert their land rights. These strategies often include the revival of traditional farming techniques and the establishment of cooperative agricultural projects that reinforce community ties and resistance against displacement. Such initiatives reflect a commitment to cultural preservation and a rejection of the erasure of their identities.

International law plays a pivotal role in framing the discourse around land rights in Palestine. The legal principles governing land ownership, occupation, and the rights of indigenous peoples provide a framework through which Palestinian communities can advocate for their rights. However, the enforcement of these laws remains inconsistent, often undermined by political interests and power dynamics that favour the status quo. Non-governmental organisations have emerged as vital actors in this landscape, working to document violations, raise awareness, and support grassroots movements that strive for justice and accountability in relation to land rights.

Media representation significantly influences public perception of land destruction in Palestinian areas, shaping narratives that either reinforce or challenge prevailing injustices. The portrayal of Palestinian agricultural practices and cultural heritage in the media can either highlight the resilience of these communities or contribute to their marginalisation. Effective storytelling that emphasises the link between cultural practices and land stewardship is essential for fostering greater understanding and support for Palestinian land rights. By connecting the struggles of Palestinian communities to broader themes of justice and cultural preservation, advocates can mobilise public opinion and drive action toward meaningful change.

International solidarity and support

INTERNATIONAL SOLIDARITY and support play a crucial role in highlighting the plight of Palestinians facing land displacement and destruction. The concept of solidarity transcends geographic boundaries, uniting diverse groups and individuals in their quest for justice and human rights. This support is vital for amplifying the voices of those affected by land loss and for fostering awareness of the ongoing challenges faced by Palestinian communities. As international actors engage with the complex realities of the region, they contribute to a broader understanding of the historical and contemporary injustices that have shaped Palestinian land rights.

The historical context of land displacement in Palestine is essential for understanding the current dynamics of struggle and resistance. From the early 20th century to the present day, various political and military actions have led to significant loss of land and the fragmentation of Palestinian communities. International solidarity movements aim to document these historical injustices, providing a narrative that counters dominant discourses that often overlook or misrepresent Palestinian experiences. By engaging with historical analyses, supporters can better articulate the need for justice and restitution, reinforcing the legitimacy of Palestinian claims to their land.

Case studies of specific Palestinian communities affected by land destruction illustrate the human impact of these policies. Through localised narratives, the experiences of families and communities facing eviction, displacement, and loss of livelihood come to the forefront. These stories not only humanise the statistics often cited in discussions about land rights but also serve as powerful tools for advocacy. International solidarity efforts that focus on these case studies can mobilise support for campaigns that demand accountability and protection for Palestinian land and rights, fostering a sense of urgency among global audiences.

Non-governmental organisations (NGOs) play a pivotal role in advocating for Palestinian land rights, often acting as intermediaries between affected communities and the international community. These organisations provide vital research, legal support, and humanitarian assistance, while also facilitating awareness-raising campaigns that highlight the impact of land destruction on Palestinian livelihoods and cultural heritage. Through collaboration with local communities, NGOs can effectively amplify their voices, ensuring that their needs and aspirations are recognised in international fora. This partnership fosters resilience among Palestinians, empowering them to continue their struggle for justice amid adversity.

Accurate and compassionate coverage can galvanise support for Palestinian rights, while biased or misleading narratives can perpetuate misunderstanding and apathy. International solidarity initiatives often seek to challenge harmful stereotypes and promote a more nuanced understanding of the situation on the ground. By advocating for fair representation and supporting independent journalism, these efforts contribute to a more informed global discourse on Palestinian land rights, ultimately fostering a climate of solidarity that is essential for meaningful change.

Chapter 16: Economic consequences of land destruction on Palestinian livelihoods

The economic structures in areas affected by land destruction in Palestine reveal a complex interplay of historical, social, and political factors that have significant implications for local communities. The ongoing thuggery, or systematic destruction of Palestinian land, has led to a profound transformation of the economic landscape. Agriculture, once the backbone of the Palestinian economy, has been severely impacted, with farmers facing restrictions on land access, loss of arable land, and damage to infrastructure. This disruption not only threatens food security but also undermines the livelihoods of families who have depended on their land for generations.

In addition to agriculture, other sectors such as trade and tourism have also been adversely affected. The imposition of movement restrictions and checkpoints has stifled local businesses, making it difficult for goods to enter and leave affected areas. This has led to a decrease in economic activity and increased unemployment rates. Local markets, which once thrived on community engagement and exchange, have become shadowed by uncertainty and fear. As businesses struggle to survive, the overall economic resilience of these communities diminishes, exacerbating the cycle of poverty and marginalisation.

Furthermore, the destruction of land has cultural and social ramifications that extend beyond immediate economic impacts. Many Palestinian communities view their land as intertwined with their identity and heritage. The loss of land not only represents a loss of physical space but also a disconnection from cultural practices and traditions that have been passed down through generations. This erosion of cultural heritage can lead to broader societal issues, including diminished community cohesion and a loss of collective memory, further complicating the economic recovery process.

Non-governmental organizations (NGOs) play a pivotal role in addressing the economic consequences of land destruction. These organisations often engage in advocacy, providing legal support and resources to affected communities. They also work on initiatives aimed at rebuilding local economies, such as promoting sustainable agricultural practices and supporting small businesses. By fostering community resilience, NGOs contribute significantly to the fight against the economic disparities exacerbated by thuggery, helping to empower communities to reclaim their rights and rebuild their livelihoods in the face of adversity.

International law offers a framework for understanding the rights of Palestinian communities regarding their land and economic resources. However, the implementation of these laws often falls short in practice, leading to continued violations and a lack of accountability for those responsible for land destruction. The intersection of law, economics, and human rights is critical in the struggle for justice in Palestine. A comprehensive analysis of the economic structures in affected areas underscores the urgent need for a concerted effort from both local and international actors to address the economic injustices faced by Palestinians and to promote sustainable development that respects their rights and heritage.

Long-term economic impacts of land loss

LONG-TERM ECONOMIC impacts of land loss in Palestine extend far beyond immediate consequences, affecting the fabric of Palestinian society and its future sustainability. The destruction of agricultural land, which has historically provided livelihoods to countless families, leads to a significant decline in local economies. As arable land diminishes, traditional farming practices are disrupted, resulting in decreased food production, increased reliance on imports, and a marked rise in food insecurity. This economic displacement not only threatens the livelihood of farmers but also reverberates through the community, as local markets face dwindling supplies and increased prices for basic goods.

Furthermore, the long-term economic impacts manifest in the form of reduced investment opportunities within affected regions. The loss of land discourages both local and foreign investment, as uncertainty about land rights and the potential for further dispossession create a climate of instability. This lack of investment stifles economic growth, leading to higher unemployment rates and a generation of youth who find fewer opportunities for meaningful employment. As communities become economically marginalised, the ability to invest in education, healthcare, and infrastructure suffers, perpetuating a cycle of poverty.

The cultural heritage of Palestinian communities is inextricably linked to their land. The long-term loss of land not only erodes economic foundations but also diminishes cultural identity. Traditional practices, crafts, and agricultural knowledge are at risk of being lost as communities are displaced and fragmented. This cultural erosion has economic implications, as the tourism sector, which relies on cultural heritage, suffers from the lack of authenticity and continuity that these communities once offered. The impact on cultural heritage further complicates efforts to rebuild local economies, as the connection between land, culture, and economic vitality is severed.

Additionally, the economic consequences of land destruction extend to the overall resilience of Palestinian communities. Communities that have lost their land face immense challenges in adapting to new economic realities. The transition from agrarian to urban economies is fraught with obstacles, including limited access to resources, inadequate infrastructure, and a lack of support systems. As these communities struggle to adapt, their overall resilience diminishes, making them more vulnerable to future shocks, whether economic or environmental. This vulnerability can lead to increased social tensions and conflict, further destabilising the region.

Finally, the role of international law and advocacy organisations becomes crucial in addressing the long-term economic impacts of land loss. Non-governmental organisations (NGOs) play a vital role in raising awareness and advocating for the rights of displaced communities. By documenting cases of land loss and promoting adherence to international legal standards, these organisations can help restore some measure of justice and support sustainable development initiatives. Ultimately, addressing the long-term economic impacts of land loss requires a multifaceted approach that includes legal advocacy, community resilience efforts, and a commitment to preserving the cultural heritage that is integral to Palestinian identity and economic stability.

Chapter 17: Cultural heritage and land loss in Palestinian history

The connection between land and Palestinian cultural identity is profound and multifaceted, deeply rooted in history, tradition, and community. For Palestinians, land is not merely a physical space; it embodies their heritage, culture, and collective memory. The historical narrative of Palestinian identity is intricately tied to specific geographic locations—homes, villages, and agricultural lands that have shaped their way of life for generations. This relationship with land is vital for understanding the ongoing struggle for rights and recognition within the context of international law and the broader Palestinian experience.

Land displacement through various forms of confiscation and destruction has had devastating effects on Palestinian communities, severing ties to ancestral properties and altering social structures. The historical analysis reveals a systematic pattern of land dispossession, often justified by political and military strategies that disregard international legal standards. As communities are uprooted, their cultural practices, agricultural traditions, and social networks are disrupted, leading to a loss of identity that transcends the physical act of displacement. The trauma associated with losing one's land extends beyond the immediate economic impacts, embedding itself into the collective psyche of displaced populations.

Case studies of specific communities highlight the diverse experiences of Palestinians affected by land destruction. For instance, the experiences of farmers in the West Bank illustrate how restrictions on land access and cultivation not only threaten their livelihoods but also their cultural expressions tied to agricultural practices. Each community's struggle encapsulates a broader narrative of resilience and resistance against erasure, demonstrating the significance of land in maintaining cultural continuity amidst ongoing challenges. These case studies reveal the intertwined nature of land rights and cultural identity, emphasising the need for a nuanced understanding of the Palestinian plight.

International law plays a critical role in framing the discourse around Palestinian land rights, providing a legal foundation for claims against displacement and destruction. The principles enshrined in various international treaties and resolutions underscore the illegality of land confiscation and the necessity of protecting cultural heritage. Non-governmental organisations have emerged as vital advocates in this regard, mobilising resources and public awareness to challenge injustices and support Palestinian communities. Their efforts not only highlight the legal dimensions of land rights but also amplify the voices of those who are often marginalised in mainstream narratives.

Media representation of land destruction in Palestinian areas serves as a powerful tool for shaping public perception and fostering empathy. The portrayal of affected communities, their struggles, and their resilience can influence international opinion and policy. Meanwhile, the economic consequences of land destruction are stark, affecting livelihoods and community stability. Yet, despite these challenges, the spirit of resilience within Palestinian communities is palpable. Cultural expressions, whether through art, music, or communal gatherings, serve as reminders of their enduring connection to the land, reinforcing the notion that their identity is not solely defined by loss but also by an unyielding commitment to reclaiming their heritage and rights.

Preservation efforts for cultural heritage sites in Palestine are critical in the context of ongoing land destruction and displacement. These sites represent not only the physical remnants of Palestinian history but also the collective identity of communities that have inhabited these lands for generations. Various organisations, both local and international, have mobilised resources to protect these sites from the effects of thuggery, which threatens not only the structures themselves but also the cultural narratives they embody. The preservation of these sites is not merely about maintaining physical locations; it is about safeguarding the memories, traditions, and histories of a people under siege.

International law recognises the importance of cultural heritage and provides a framework for its protection. Instruments such as the Hague Convention for the Protection of Cultural Property in the Event of Armed Conflict emphasise the responsibility of states to safeguard cultural sites during times of conflict. However, the application of these laws in Palestine remains problematic. The lack of effective enforcement mechanisms, combined with the political complexities on the ground, often leaves these laws unheeded. As a result, cultural heritage sites are frequently at risk of destruction, further eroding the sense of identity and continuity for Palestinian communities.

Non-governmental organisations play a pivotal role in the preservation of Palestinian cultural heritage. By documenting sites at risk and advocating for their protection, these organisations raise awareness of the ongoing threats to Palestinian history. Initiatives such as restoration projects, educational programs, and community engagement efforts are vital in fostering a sense of ownership and pride among local communities. These organisations also facilitate international advocacy, mobilising support from the global community to pressure authorities to respect cultural heritage protections.

Media representation of cultural heritage preservation efforts is also crucial in shaping public perception and understanding of the situation in Palestine. Coverage that highlights the significance of cultural sites and the threats they face can galvanise support for preservation initiatives. Conversely, narratives that ignore or downplay the cultural dimensions of land destruction contribute to the erasure of Palestinian identity and history. It is essential for media outlets to provide nuanced reporting that recognises the intersection of cultural heritage and land rights.

Ultimately, the preservation of cultural heritage sites in Palestine is intertwined with the broader struggle for land rights and justice. As communities continue to resist displacement and advocate for their rights, the protection of their cultural heritage becomes a powerful symbol of resilience. These efforts not only honour the past but also assert the future of Palestinian identity, reinforcing the notion that cultural heritage is an integral part of the fight for justice and recognition on the international stage.

The role of education in cultural resilience is crucial for communities facing the challenges of land displacement and destruction, particularly in the context of Palestine. Education serves as a foundation for the preservation of cultural identity, enabling individuals to understand their history, heritage, and the significance of their land. In Palestinian communities, educational initiatives that focus on local history and cultural practices empower individuals to resist erasure and maintain their connection to the land. This understanding cultivates a sense of belonging and solidarity among community members, reinforcing their collective identity even in the face of adversity.

Moreover, education can be a powerful tool for advocating land rights and raising awareness about the legal frameworks that govern such issues. By incorporating lessons on international law and human rights into curricula, Palestinian educators can equip students with the knowledge necessary to challenge injustices related to land displacement. This education fosters critical thinking and encourages youth to engage in activism, ensuring that they are not merely passive victims of circumstance but active participants in the struggle for their rights.

Community-based educational programs also play a significant role in fostering resilience. These programs often emphasise traditional practices, storytelling, and the transmission of cultural knowledge from one generation to another. By revitalising these practices, communities can reinforce their cultural heritage and instil a sense of pride among younger generations. This intergenerational transfer of knowledge is essential for sustaining cultural identity, especially in regions where external forces seek to undermine or obliterate it.

Non-governmental organisations (NGOs) often collaborate with local communities to enhance educational efforts, focusing on both formal and informal education. NGOs can provide resources, training, and support to educators, enabling them to create curricula that reflect the realities faced by Palestinian communities. These partnerships not only strengthen educational initiatives but also promote community engagement and advocacy, ensuring that the voices of Palestinians are heard in broader discussions about land rights and cultural heritage.

Finally, the integration of education into community resilience strategies is vital for fostering hope and agency among Palestinians. Education not only informs individuals about their rights but also inspires them to envision a future where their cultural identities are preserved and their land rights respected. As Palestinian communities continue to navigate the impacts of land destruction and displacement, education stands as a beacon of resilience, equipping them with the tools necessary to confront challenges and advocate for justice.

Chapter 18: Conclusion: Pathways to justice for Palestinian land rights

Summary of Key Findings

The examination of Palestinian land rights within the framework of international law reveals a profound neglect of these rights, characterised by systematic violations and a lack of accountability for those responsible. Key findings indicate that the phenomenon of thuggery is not merely an isolated occurrence but part of a broader strategy that undermines the socio-economic fabric of Palestinian communities. Historical analysis demonstrates a consistent pattern of land displacement that has evolved over decades, often justified under various legal pretences, yet fundamentally rooted in political agendas that disregard the fundamental rights of the Palestinian people.

Case studies of specific Palestinian communities illustrate the tangible effects of land destruction. For instance, the village of Susiya has faced repeated demolitions of structures and the appropriation of agricultural land, which has severely impacted the livelihood of its residents. These localised instances highlight a disturbing trend where international legal standards are flouted, and communities are left vulnerable to ongoing encroachments. The resilience exhibited by these communities in the face of adversity underscores the importance of grassroots advocacy and the need for continued support from external sources.

International law provides a framework for protecting land rights, yet its application in the context of Palestine has been inconsistent and often ineffective. The findings suggest that while various resolutions and declarations affirm the rights of Palestinians to their land, the lack of enforcement mechanisms allows violations to persist. Non-governmental organisations play a crucial role in advocating for these rights, documenting violations, and raising awareness at both local and international levels. Their efforts are vital in drawing attention to the plight of affected communities and mobilising support for justice.

Media representation of land destruction in Palestinian areas often shapes public perception and influences policy responses. The key findings indicate that coverage can vary significantly, with some narratives focusing on the human impact of land loss, while others may perpetuate stereotypes or overlook the historical context of the conflict. This disparity in representation emphasises the need for responsible journalism that accurately portrays the realities faced by Palestinians and fosters a more informed public discourse.

The economic consequences of land destruction extend beyond immediate loss of property; they ripple through the broader Palestinian economy, affecting livelihoods and community sustainability. Cultural heritage is deeply intertwined with land, and the ongoing loss of territory threatens the historical legacy and identity of Palestinian communities. As resilience efforts take shape, it becomes clear that addressing these multifaceted challenges requires a comprehensive approach that not only advocates for rights but also seeks to preserve the cultural integrity and economic viability of Palestinian society.

Recommendations for policy and advocacy

TO EFFECTIVELY ADDRESS the ongoing challenges related to Palestinian land rights and the destructive practices of thuggery, it is essential for policymakers and advocates to develop comprehensive strategies that prioritise justice and accountability. One of the primary recommendations is to strengthen international legal frameworks that protect land rights. This can be achieved by urging states to ratify and implement relevant international treaties that uphold the rights of indigenous populations and ensure the protection of their lands from unlawful occupation and destruction. Advocacy efforts should focus on promoting the enforcement of these laws through international bodies, such as the United Nations, to hold violators accountable and provide support for affected communities.

Engagement with non-governmental organisations (NGOs) plays a crucial role in amplifying the voices of Palestinian communities and advocating for their land rights. NGOs can serve as vital intermediaries, facilitating communication between affected communities and international stakeholders.

Recommendations include increasing funding for these organisations to enhance their capacity for advocacy, legal support, and community education. Additionally, forming coalitions among NGOs focused on land rights can strengthen their collective impact, allowing them to share resources, expertise, and strategies to address the complex issues surrounding thuggery and land displacement.

Media representation is another critical area for advocacy efforts. The portrayal of Palestinian land loss in the media often lacks nuance and fails to convey the historical and cultural significance of these lands to the Palestinian people. Advocacy should aim to work with journalists and media outlets to promote in-depth reporting that highlights personal stories, historical contexts, and the broader implications of land destruction. This includes creating partnerships with media organisations to support narratives that reflect the resilience of Palestinian communities and their ongoing efforts to reclaim and protect their land.

Moreover, it is essential to foster community resilience in the face of land loss. Policymakers and advocates should prioritise the development of programs that empower Palestinian communities economically and socially. This can include initiatives that promote sustainable agricultural practices, support local businesses, and provide access to education and healthcare. By investing in community-led solutions, advocates can help mitigate the economic consequences of land destruction and support the preservation of cultural heritage, which is often closely tied to the land.

Finally, engaging with international and regional human rights mechanisms is pivotal for advocating Palestinian land rights. This involves submitting reports to human rights bodies, participating in public hearings, and utilising the Universal Periodic Review process to bring attention to violations associated with thuggery and land destruction. By raising awareness at these levels, advocates can pressure governments to take action and influence public opinion, thereby fostering a more informed dialogue surrounding Palestinian land rights and promoting a just resolution to the ongoing struggle for sovereignty and recognition.

Future directions for research and activism

The future directions for research and activism regarding Palestinian land rights must focus on a multifaceted approach that addresses the complex layers of historical, legal, and social issues surrounding land displacement. Scholars and activists should prioritise comprehensive historical analyses that document the long-term impacts of thuggery on Palestinian land. This research should not only chronicle past events but also examine the evolving legal frameworks that govern land rights in Palestine. A deeper understanding of historical injustices can help frame current advocacy efforts, providing a robust foundation for claims of rights and restitution.

Case studies of specific Palestinian communities affected by thuggery will be essential in illuminating the unique challenges faced by different groups. By focusing on localised impacts, researchers can create detailed narratives that highlight individual and community resilience. These case studies should incorporate perspectives from affected residents and document their strategies for survival and resistance. By showcasing diverse experiences, this work can serve as a powerful tool for advocacy, demonstrating the urgent need for international attention and support for these communities.

International law remains a critical area for engagement, particularly in how it relates to land rights in Palestine. Future research should analyse the effectiveness of existing legal frameworks and explore potential avenues for reform. This includes evaluating the role of international organisations and treaties in protecting Palestinian land rights and holding violators accountable. Activists can leverage this research to press for stronger enforcement mechanisms and increased compliance from states and multinational entities involved in land acquisition or destruction.

Non-governmental organizations (NGOs) play a pivotal role in advocating for Palestinian land rights and should continue to expand their efforts in both research and activism. Collaboration among NGOs can enhance resource sharing and amplify advocacy efforts. Future directions should also include the establishment of networks that facilitate knowledge exchange between local activists and international supporters. These networks can help build a cohesive strategy that addresses both grassroots needs and broader geopolitical concerns, ensuring that the voices of affected communities are heard on global platforms.

Media representation is another crucial area that demands attention. Research should focus on how narratives surrounding Palestinian land destruction are framed in various media outlets, and how these frames influence public perception and policy. Activists must engage in strategic communication campaigns that highlight the cultural heritage and historical significance of Palestinian land. By fostering a deeper understanding of the economic and cultural ramifications of land loss, advocates can mobilise broader public support for restoration efforts and policy changes that prioritise justice for Palestinian communities.

Chapter 19: The price of peace: Analysing the aftermath of the October 7th attack

Chapter 1: The Prelude to Conflict

The historical context of Israeli-Palestinian relations is crucial for understanding the complexities surrounding the conflict, particularly in light of recent events such as the October 7th attack by Hamas. The roots of this conflict can be traced back to the late 19th and early 20th centuries, with the rise of nationalist movements among both Jews and Arabs. The Zionist movement sought to establish a Jewish homeland in Palestine, a region that was predominantly Arab at the time. This goal led to increasing tensions between Jewish immigrants and the Arab population, setting the stage for future conflict.

The British Mandate for Palestine, established after World War I, further complicated the situation. The Balfour Declaration of 1917 expressed British support for the establishment of a Jewish national home in Palestine, which was met with resistance from the Arab community. This period saw a series of violent clashes between Jews and Arabs, exacerbating mutual distrust and animosity. The culmination of this conflict occurred in 1948 with the establishment of the State of Israel, which was followed by the Arab-Israeli War. This war resulted in significant territorial changes and the displacement of hundreds of thousands of Palestinians, creating a refugee crisis that continues to impact relations to this day.

In the decades following Israel's founding, the conflict evolved through several key events, including the Six-Day War in 1967, during which Israel captured the West Bank, Gaza Strip, and East Jerusalem. This occupation intensified Palestinian resistance and led to the emergence of the Palestinian Liberation Organization (PLO) as a representative body. The late 20th century witnessed attempts at peace, such as the Oslo Accords in the 1990s, which aimed to establish a framework for a two-state solution. However, these efforts were undermined by ongoing violence, settlement expansion, and political fragmentation within both Israeli and Palestinian societies.

The second intifada, which erupted in 2000, marked a significant escalation of violence and further entrenched divisions between the two groups. Hamas, an Islamist militant group, gained prominence during this period, advocating for armed resistance against Israeli occupation. The 2006 elections, which resulted in Hamas taking control of Gaza, led to a split in governance between Hamas in Gaza and the Fatah-led Palestinian Authority in the West Bank. This division has complicated peace efforts and created distinct political realities that hinder cooperation and dialogue.

The aftermath of the October 7th attack by Hamas has reignited longstanding grievances and prompted renewed military responses from Israel, including widespread bombings in Gaza. This escalation raises questions about the future of peace in the region, as it underscores the cycle of violence that has characterised Israeli-Palestinian relations for decades. Understanding this historical context is essential for grasping the current dynamics and the profound challenges that lie ahead in the pursuit of a sustainable resolution to the conflict.

Overview of Hamas and its objectives

HAMAS, AN ACRONYM FOR Harakat al-Muqawama al-Islamiyya, emerged in the late 1980s during the First Intifada as an offshoot of the Egyptian Muslim Brotherhood. Its founding charter, released in 1988, emphasised the organisation's commitment to the liberation of Palestine through armed struggle and the establishment of an Islamic state in the territory of historic Palestine. Over the years, Hamas has evolved into a multifaceted organization, incorporating social, political, and military dimensions. While it operates primarily in the Gaza Strip, its influence extends to the West Bank and the broader Palestinian diaspora.

The objectives of Hamas are rooted in its ideological framework, which centres on resistance against Israeli occupation and the pursuit of Palestinian self-determination. The organisation views itself as a defender of Palestinian rights and sovereignty, promoting the narrative that armed resistance is a legitimate response to perceived oppression. This perspective has garnered significant support among Palestinians, particularly in areas where the socio-economic conditions are dire. Hamas positions itself not only as a political entity but also as a social movement, providing essential services such as education, healthcare, and welfare to many Gazans.

In the aftermath of the October 7th attack, Hamas's strategic objectives have come under intense scrutiny. The attack, characterised by a sudden and coordinated assault on Israeli territory, marked a significant escalation in the ongoing conflict. Hamas aimed to demonstrate its military capabilities and reassert its relevance within the Palestinian political landscape, particularly in light of diminishing support for the Palestinian Authority in the West Bank. The timing and scale of the operation suggest that Hamas intended to shift the dynamics of the Israeli-Palestinian conflict, forcing a recalibration of international attention and engagement.

Hamas's military wing, the Izz ad-Din al-Qassam Brigades, plays a crucial role in the organisation's operations, employing tactics that range from rocket fire to tunnel warfare. The group's military capabilities have evolved significantly over the years, allowing it to inflict damage on Israeli targets and challenge the perception of invulnerability associated with the Israeli defence Forces. This military posture is not only a means of resistance but also a tool for internal propaganda, reinforcing Hamas's image as a formidable force against Israel and rallying support among Palestinians.

The international community's response to Hamas and its objectives is complex and often contentious. Many countries classify Hamas as a terrorist organization, complicating efforts for dialogue and reconciliation. However, some argue that understanding Hamas's motivations and the socio-political context of its actions is essential for any meaningful peace process. As the aftermath of the October 7th attack unfolds, the challenge remains for both Israeli and Palestinian leaders to navigate the intricate landscape shaped by Hamas's objectives and the broader quest for peace in the region.

The events leading up to October 7th

THE EVENTS LEADING up to October 7th were marked by escalating tensions between Israel and Hamas, rooted in a complex history of conflict, territorial disputes, and political strife. In the months preceding the attack, there were numerous signs indicating a deterioration in relations. Incidents of violence, including rocket fire from Gaza into Israeli territory and retaliatory airstrikes, became increasingly frequent. These skirmishes served as a precursor to the more significant and coordinated events that would unfold on that fateful day.

In the weeks leading up to the attack, Hamas intensified its rhetoric against Israel, framing its narratives around resistance and the defence of Palestinian rights. This period saw heightened propaganda efforts, aiming to galvanise support both domestically and among sympathisers abroad. The organisation sought to portray itself as the defender of the Palestinian cause, utilising social media and public statements to rally their base and emphasise the perceived injustices faced by Palestinians in Gaza and the West Bank.

Simultaneously, Israel's military strategy in the region became more assertive, reflecting a zero-tolerance approach to any form of aggression. The Israeli government responded to the increasing rocket fire with targeted operations aimed at dismantling Hamas' military capabilities. These operations, however, were often met with international scrutiny, as civilian casualties mounted and humanitarian concerns grew. The situation thus created a volatile environment, wherein both parties perceived their actions as essential for national security, further entrenching the cycle of violence.

Diplomatic efforts to de-escalate the situation were largely ineffective, with various international entities attempting to mediate the conflict. However, these attempts often fell short due to the deep-seated mistrust between the parties involved. The lack of significant progress in peace negotiations contributed to a sense of hopelessness on both sides, with many Palestinians feeling marginalised and Israelis fearing for their security. This backdrop of despair and aggression set the stage for the catastrophic events of October 7th.

On that day, the culmination of these tensions erupted into a large-scale assault by Hamas, characterised by a surprise attack that caught Israeli forces off guard. The scale and coordination of the operation marked a significant escalation in hostilities and led to devastating consequences for both sides. The aftermath of the attack would not only reshape the landscape of Israeli-Palestinian relations but also prompt a significant military response from Israel, which would have lasting implications for the region and beyond.

Description of the attack

THE OCTOBER 7TH ATTACK, executed by Hamas, marked a pivotal moment in the ongoing conflict between Israel and Palestinian groups. In the early hours of that day, a coordinated assault unfolded that involved a barrage of rockets launched from Gaza into Israeli territory. Over 3,000 rockets were fired within a short span, overwhelming the Iron Dome defence system, which, while highly effective, could not intercept every missile. This unprecedented scale of aerial bombardment caught Israel off guard and set the stage for a profound escalation in hostilities.

In addition to the rocket attacks, ground incursions by Hamas militants breached the Israeli border, leading to direct confrontations with Israeli defence Forces (IDF). Armed groups infiltrated civilian areas, targeting towns and communities in a shocking display of aggression. Reports indicated that militants engaged in acts of violence against civilians, including hostage-taking and mass shootings, creating a climate of fear that reverberated throughout the nation. The tactical execution of the attack showcased a significant level of planning and coordination, highlighting Hamas's capabilities in asymmetric warfare.

The immediate aftermath of the attack saw Israel mobilising its military forces in response to the unprecedented threat. The IDF launched extensive airstrikes targeting Hamas infrastructure in Gaza, including command centres, weapon storage facilities, and launch sites. As the bombings intensified, civilian casualties in Gaza began to rise, leading to a humanitarian crisis that drew international concern. The Israeli government justified these actions as necessary for national security, arguing that the elimination of Hamas's operational capabilities was crucial to prevent future attacks.

The global reaction to the October 7th attack and the subsequent Israeli response was polarised. Supporters of Israel viewed the military action as a legitimate defence against terrorism, while critics raised alarms over the humanitarian impact on the Palestinian population. Protests erupted worldwide, with demonstrations in support of both sides illustrating the deep divisions within international perspectives on the conflict. The narrative surrounding the attacks became a focal point for discussions about morality, justice, and the implications of military responses in densely populated areas.

As the situation developed, the long-term consequences of the October 7th attack began to unfold. The cycles of violence and retaliation raised questions about the feasibility of peace negotiations and the potential for a lasting resolution to the Israeli-Palestinian conflict. The attack not only reshaped the tactical landscape of the region but also influenced political discourse both locally and internationally. As each side fortified its position, the prospect of dialogue seemed increasingly remote, underscoring the complexities and challenges inherent in achieving peace in a deeply fragmented context.

The immediate reactions to the October 7th attack by Hamas were marked by a profound sense of shock and outrage within Israel and among its allies. News of the assault spread rapidly, igniting a wave of condemnation from various quarters. Israeli officials described the attack as an unprecedented act of terrorism, leading to emergency meetings among security and military leaders. The scale and brutality of the assault caught many off guard, prompting immediate calls for a robust response to ensure national security and deter future attacks.

In the hours following the attack, social media became a battleground for narratives surrounding the event. Israeli citizens expressed their anger, fear, and grief online, while also rallying support for the military response anticipated from their government. This digital outpouring reflected a collective need for solidarity in the face of violence, as many citizens shared personal stories and images that underscored the human impact of the attack. The emotional weight of the situation was palpable, further intensifying the public's demand for justice and security.

The Israeli government swiftly mobilised its military forces, launching airstrikes in Gaza as part of its immediate response. The aim was to target Hamas infrastructure and leadership while signalling to both domestic and international audiences that Israel would not tolerate such aggression. The airstrikes, characterised by their intensity and frequency, were framed as a necessary measure to restore deterrence and protect civilians from future threats. However, this military strategy sparked a broader debate regarding the consequences of such actions, particularly in terms of civilian casualties and the potential for escalating conflict.

International reactions varied, with many countries expressing support for Israel's right to defend itself against terrorism. However, there were also calls for restraint, emphasising the importance of minimising civilian suffering in Gaza. Humanitarian organizations began voicing concerns about the potential humanitarian crisis that could unfold as a result of the military response. The discourse around the conflict became increasingly polarised, with various factions advocating for different approaches to achieving peace and security in the region.

As days turned into weeks following the attack, the ramifications of the initial reactions became evident. The Israeli public remained deeply affected by the events, leading to increased vigilance and heightened security measures across the country. Simultaneously, the international community grappled with the implications of the conflict, as discussions about long-term solutions and the necessity of addressing the underlying issues between Israelis and Palestinians gained prominence. The immediate responses to the October 7th attack set the stage for a complex and evolving narrative about peace, security, and the human costs of conflict in the region.

International reactions

INTERNATIONAL REACTIONS to the events following the October 7th attack by Hamas have been diverse and complex, reflecting a wide range of geopolitical interests and humanitarian concerns. Countries and organisations around the world responded with statements that emphasised their positions on the conflict, the right to self-defence, and the need for humanitarian aid. The attack, which resulted in significant casualties and destruction, led to a swift military response from Israel, prompting debates about proportionality and the rules of engagement in armed conflict.

The United States, a staunch ally of Israel, expressed unequivocal support for Israel's right to defend itself against what it termed a terrorist attack. U.S. officials emphasised the importance of Israel's security and condemned Hamas's actions as unprovoked aggression. This support was reflected in military aid commitments and diplomatic backing at various international forums. However, the U.S. also faced pressure from human rights organisations and some lawmakers to address the humanitarian implications of Israel's military response, calling for measures to protect civilians in Gaza.

European nations exhibited a more varied response, with some governments voicing strong support for Israel while also urging restraint to prevent civilian casualties. The European Union collectively called for de-escalation and emphasised the necessity of protecting civilians and ensuring access to humanitarian aid. Countries like Germany and France reiterated their support for Israel's right to defend itself but also highlighted the urgent need to address the humanitarian crisis that unfolded as a result of the military actions in Gaza.

In the Middle East, reactions were predictably charged, with many Arab nations expressing solidarity with the Palestinian cause. Leaders from countries such as Turkey and Iran condemned Israel's military actions, framing them as acts of aggression against the Palestinian people. Regional organisations, like the Arab League, convened to discuss a coordinated response, emphasising a collective call for an immediate ceasefire and the initiation of peace talks aimed at resolving the underlying issues of the Israeli-Palestinian conflict. The rhetoric often reflected long-standing grievances and the broader geopolitical struggles in the region.

International organisations, including the United Nations, called for an urgent investigation into the events and the humanitarian impact of the conflict. The UN emphasised the importance of adhering to international law and protecting civilian lives during armed conflict. Humanitarian organisations raised alarms about the escalating humanitarian crisis in Gaza, calling for immediate access to aid and medical assistance for those affected. The international community's reactions underscored the complexities of the situation, highlighting the balance between national security concerns and the urgent need for humanitarian intervention.

As I write these few pages on this very topic, (May 2025) every bit of food aid, medicine, truck-loads of supplies have been halted for weeks and not allowed through to the starving Palestinians. Water, electricity etc are all cut off and so, with all fairness, this is creating a humanitarian catastrophe while the world seats quietly.

Chapter 20: The Israeli response

Military strategy and operations

Military strategy and operations in the aftermath of the October 7th attack by Hamas have been pivotal in shaping Israel's response and the broader conflict dynamics in the region. The attack, which resulted in significant civilian casualties and damage, prompted Israel to reassess its security framework and military posture. In light of these events, the Israeli defence Forces (IDF) initiated a series of operations aimed at both immediate retaliation and long-term strategic deterrence. This military response is characterised by a combination of aerial bombardments, ground operations, and intelligence-driven actions designed to dismantle Hamas's infrastructure and capabilities.

The military strategy employed by Israel following the attack can be broadly categorised into three key objectives: neutralising immediate threats, degrading enemy capabilities, and establishing a sustained deterrent posture. The immediate response involved targeted airstrikes aimed at high-value Hamas targets, including command centres, weapon storage facilities, and operational leaders. These strikes were meticulously planned based on intelligence assessments to minimise civilian casualties while maximising operational effectiveness. The use of precision-guided munitions and advanced surveillance systems underscored Israel's commitment to minimising collateral damage while achieving strategic goals.

In addition to aerial operations, Israel's ground strategy has also evolved. The IDF launched ground incursions into Gaza to root out Hamas fighters and infrastructure directly. These operations were informed by intelligence gathered from various sources, including human intelligence and surveillance drones. Ground forces operated in tandem with air support, utilising a combined arms approach that aimed to overwhelm Hamas's defensive positions. This strategy also included the establishment of buffer zones to protect Israeli territory from further attacks, demonstrating a dual focus on immediate military objectives and long-term security needs.

Another critical aspect of Israel's military strategy has been the emphasis on psychological operations and information warfare. In the wake of the October 7th attack, Israel recognised the importance of countering Hamas's narrative and maintaining domestic and international support for its actions. This involved disseminating information about the operational goals and justifications for military actions, as well as highlighting the humanitarian measures taken to mitigate civilian impact. By framing its military operations within a narrative of self-defence and preserving national security, Israel aimed to bolster its legitimacy on the world stage while also reassuring its own populace.

Lastly, the long-term implications of Israel's military strategy post-October 7th extend beyond immediate operational concerns. The effectiveness of these strategies will likely influence future relations with Hamas and the broader Palestinian population, as well as Israel's standing in the international community. Ongoing military operations must be balanced with diplomatic efforts to address the underlying conflict dynamics, as unilateral military actions can sometimes exacerbate tensions and hinder peace initiatives. Therefore, while military strategy and operations play a crucial role in Israel's response, they must be integrated within a broader framework that seeks lasting peace and stability in the region.

Civilian impact and casualties

THE AFTERMATH OF THE October 7th attack by Hamas has had profound implications for civilians, particularly in the context of the military responses that followed. The immediate impact on civilian populations is often a tragic consequence of warfare, and the Israeli bombings post-attack are no exception. As military operations escalated, communities found themselves caught in the crossfire, facing loss of life, displacement, and destruction of infrastructure. The civilian toll in such conflicts is a critical aspect that must be examined to fully understand the human cost of military engagements.

In the days following the attack, Israeli airstrikes targeted areas in Gaza, which were believed to be staging grounds for Hamas operations. However, these strikes inevitably led to significant civilian casualties. Reports indicated that many of those killed were non-combatants, including women and children, who bore the brunt of the violence. The high number of civilian fatalities has sparked international outrage and calls for accountability, raising questions about the proportionality and necessity of military actions in densely populated areas.

The destruction of homes, schools, and hospitals further exacerbated the humanitarian crisis. With infrastructure severely damaged, essential services such as healthcare and education faced overwhelming challenges. Many families were forced to flee their homes, leading to a surge in internally displaced persons. The United Nations and various humanitarian organisations reported a critical need for aid, as the situation deteriorated rapidly. The psychological impact of such violence on civilians, particularly children, cannot be understated, as trauma from witnessing violence or losing loved ones can have long-lasting effects.

International responses to the civilian impact of the bombings have varied, with some governments condemning the loss of innocent lives while others defended Israel's right to retaliate. This disparity in responses can influence public perception and policy, which complicates the narrative surrounding the conflict. The complexities of international law, particularly concerning the protection of civilians in armed conflict, come into sharper focus as the situation unfolds. Identifying accountability for any violations of international humanitarian law becomes imperative in the pursuit of justice for affected civilians.

In conclusion, the civilian impact and casualties resulting from the Israeli bombing after the October 7th attack highlight the tragic consequences of military conflict. Evaluating these outcomes is essential for understanding the broader implications of warfare in populated areas. The need for a balanced approach that prioritises civilian safety and adheres to international humanitarian standards is crucial in mitigating future tragedies. As the region continues to grapple with the aftermath, the voices of civilians must be amplified to ensure that their experiences and needs are recognised and addressed in any ongoing discussions about peace and security.

Political implications within Israel

THE IMMEDIATE AFTERMATH saw a surge in national security rhetoric, with government officials asserting the need for a robust military response. This response was not only aimed at Hamas but also at the broader Palestinian community, which many Israelis began to view with increased suspicion. The attack reignited debates surrounding Israeli-Palestinian relations, security policies, and the role of military action in achieving long-term peace. As the government rallied public support for an aggressive military strategy, there was a palpable shift in the political landscape, with various factions vying for influence in the wake of the crisis.

In the wake of the attack, the Israeli political spectrum experienced a realignment, with right-wing parties gaining prominence. The attack provided a significant boost to hardline political factions that advocate for a more aggressive stance towards Hamas and a more assertive military presence in Gaza. This shift has implications for the balance of power within the Knesset, potentially sidelining centrist and leftist parties that traditionally support negotiations and peace initiatives. The public's fear and anger following the attack have created an environment where calls for strong military action resonate more than diplomatic outreach, thereby complicating the possibility of future peace talks.

The reaction to the attack has also highlighted the challenges of governance in Israel, particularly regarding the internal divisions among its citizens. The Jewish population has largely rallied around the government's military response, while Arab citizens of Israel have expressed concerns over the implications of such a stance on their communities. This division poses a significant challenge for Israeli leaders, who must navigate the delicate balance between national security and the need for social cohesion. The potential marginalisation of Arab citizens in political discourse could lead to increased tensions and further complicate the already fraught relations between Jewish and Arab populations within Israel.

Additionally, the international response to the October 7th attack has influenced Israel's political landscape. The United States and other Western allies have generally supported Israel's right to defend itself, which has emboldened the current government to pursue a more aggressive military strategy. However, this support is not without its critics, both domestically and internationally. Calls for restraint and concern over civilian casualties in Gaza have prompted some within Israel to question the sustainability of a purely military approach. This internal dissent may lead to shifts in public opinion, potentially impacting future elections and policy decisions.

Ultimately, the political implications within Israel following the October 7th attack by Hamas reflect a complex interplay of security, governance, and societal dynamics. As the country grapples with the aftermath of violence, the direction of its political future remains uncertain. The emphasis on military solutions may provide short-term security, but the long-term implications for Israeli democracy, social unity, and the quest for peace with the Palestinians remain to be seen. The decisions made in this critical period will resonate well beyond the immediate response to the attack, shaping the contours of Israeli politics for years to come.

Chapter 21: The humanitarian crisis

Displacement and refugees

The aftermath of the October 7th attack by Hamas has led to a significant increase in displacement within the region, particularly affecting Palestinian communities in Gaza. The escalation of violence has forced thousands to flee their homes in search of safety, exacerbating an already dire humanitarian situation. The bombardment by Israeli forces in response to the attack has further intensified the crisis, with many civilians caught in the crossfire. This has resulted in a large-scale displacement of families, leading to overcrowded shelters and a strain on already limited resources.

As the conflict continues, the number of refugees seeking shelter both within Gaza and in neighbouring countries has surged. Many families have been separated in the chaos, compounding their trauma and making it difficult to access basic necessities such as food, water, and medical care. The international community has been called upon to respond to this growing humanitarian crisis, but the logistics of delivering aid amid ongoing hostilities pose significant challenges. Humanitarian organisations are struggling to reach those in need, and the risk of further violence complicates their efforts.

The impact of displacement extends beyond immediate survival needs. Families uprooted from their homes face psychological challenges, including trauma and anxiety, stemming from their experiences during the attacks. Children, in particular, are vulnerable to long-term psychological effects, which can hinder their development and well-being. As the situation continues to unfold, the need for mental health support and trauma-informed care becomes increasingly critical in addressing the broader implications of displacement.

Moreover, the displacement crisis raises questions about the future of these communities. As families find themselves in temporary shelters or none of it, the uncertainty regarding their return home looms large. The destruction of infrastructure in heavily bombed areas means that even if the conflict were to cease, returning home may not be feasible for many. The long-term prospects for rebuilding and recovery are daunting, and the potential for a protracted refugee situation looms, with implications for regional stability and international relations.

In conclusion, the displacement and refugee crisis following the October 7th attack is an issue that requires urgent attention. Addressing the immediate needs of those affected is crucial, but so too is the need for a comprehensive approach to ensure long-term support and recovery. The international community must prioritise humanitarian aid, engage in diplomatic efforts to resolve the conflict, and develop strategies to address the root causes of displacement to foster a sustainable peace in the region.

Access to basic necessities

ACCESS TO BASIC NECESSITIES in the aftermath of the October 7th attack has become a critical issue in Israel and the surrounding regions. The escalation of conflict has significantly disrupted the supply chains and access to essential resources, including food, water, medical supplies, and shelter. As the situation evolves, the humanitarian implications are profound, affecting not only those directly involved in the conflict but also the broader population that relies on stable access to these necessities for survival and well-being.

In the immediate wake of the attack, infrastructure damage due to bombing campaigns has severely impacted the ability to deliver vital resources. Many roads, bridges, and supply routes have been compromised, complicating logistics for humanitarian aid organisations. Essential services, including healthcare facilities, have been overwhelmed or rendered inoperative, limiting access to medical care for those injured in the conflict and those with chronic health conditions. This disruption has created a dire situation where the most vulnerable populations are at an increased risk of suffering from preventable diseases and injuries.

Water scarcity has emerged as a pressing concern, exacerbated by damage to water distribution systems and contamination of water sources. Many communities are facing acute shortages, leading to reliance on bottled water or unregulated sources that pose health risks. The lack of clean water not only affects daily living conditions but also has broader implications for sanitation and hygiene, which are critical for preventing outbreaks of disease. As the bombing continues, the restoration of water services and the establishment of reliable access to potable water is becoming increasingly urgent.

Food insecurity is another significant challenge that has arisen in the context of the ongoing conflict. Agricultural production has been severely disrupted, with farms and food supply chains suffering losses due to violence and instability. The price of basic food items has skyrocketed, making it difficult for families to afford essential nutrition. In some areas, local markets have been closed or destroyed, forcing residents to rely on external aid, which is often inconsistent and insufficient to meet the needs of the population. As the humanitarian crisis deepens, the international community is faced with the challenge of delivering food assistance amid ongoing hostilities.

Efforts to address these crises must be multifaceted, focusing not only on immediate relief but also on long-term recovery and rebuilding. Humanitarian organisations are mobilising to provide emergency assistance, including food distribution, medical care, and water purification efforts. However, sustained access to basic necessities will require a concerted effort from local and international actors to negotiate ceasefires, ensure safe passage for aid workers, and restore critical infrastructure. Without significant intervention, the cycle of deprivation and violence is likely to continue, further complicating the path toward peace and stability in the region.

Health care in Israel has faced significant challenges in the aftermath of the October 7th attack by Hamas. The immediate impact of the assault resulted in a surge of casualties, overwhelming medical facilities and personnel. Hospitals in affected areas were quickly filled to capacity, struggling to provide adequate care for those injured during the attack. Emergency services were stretched thin, with first responders working tirelessly under extreme pressure to save lives. This unprecedented influx of patients highlighted not only the immediate health care needs but also the vulnerabilities within the health care system itself.

In addition to the physical injuries sustained during the attack, the psychological toll on both the victims and the broader population poses another serious challenge. Many individuals experienced trauma from the violence, leading to increased demand for mental health services. The stress and anxiety related to ongoing security threats have further complicated the mental well-being of citizens. Mental health professionals are now faced with the task of addressing both acute psychological emergencies and long-term mental health care for individuals grappling with the aftermath of violence. The need for accessible mental health resources has become paramount as communities seek to rebuild and recover.

Moreover, the ongoing conflict has disrupted routine health care services. Patients with chronic conditions have found it increasingly difficult to access necessary medications and treatments. The instability in the region has led to interruptions in supply chains, affecting the availability of essential pharmaceuticals and medical equipment. Health care providers are now tasked with finding alternative solutions to ensure that patients continue to receive the care they require, even in a climate of uncertainty. These disruptions have long-term implications for public health, as untreated conditions can lead to further complications down the line.

The economic strain on the health care system cannot be overlooked either. Increased military expenditures have diverted funds away from health care initiatives, exacerbating existing disparities in access to care. As resources become limited, health care providers may struggle to maintain the quality of care they can offer. Additionally, the workforce is impacted, as many health care professionals may experience burnout or choose to leave the region due to safety concerns. The sustainability of the health care system hinges on the ability to adapt to these economic pressures while still meeting the needs of the population.

Finally, addressing these health care challenges requires a coordinated response from both governmental and non-governmental organizations. Collaborative efforts will be essential in rebuilding the health care infrastructure and ensuring that all citizens have access to necessary services. Initiatives aimed at improving resilience within the health care system, enhancing mental health support, and ensuring a steady supply of medical resources will be crucial in the recovery process. The path forward demands not only immediate action but also a long-term commitment to fostering a robust health care system capable of withstanding future crises.

Chapter 22: Global reactions and responses

International organisations play a crucial role in shaping responses to conflicts and crises, particularly in the aftermath of the October 7th attack by Hamas on Israel. Organisations such as the United Nations (UN), the European Union (EU), and various non-governmental organisations (NGOs) are often at the forefront of efforts to mediate disputes, provide humanitarian aid, and promote peace. Following the escalation of violence, these entities have been tasked with navigating a complex geopolitical landscape, seeking to ensure that humanitarian needs are met while also addressing the underlying causes of conflict.

The UN has a longstanding mandate in addressing international peace and security issues. In the wake of the October 7th attack, the UN Security Council convened to discuss the situation, with member states debating potential resolutions aimed at de-escalation. The organisation has also called for investigations into the attacks and subsequent military responses, emphasising the importance of accountability. Through its agencies, such as the UN Relief and Works Agency for Palestine Refugees (UNRWA), the UN works to provide essential services and support to those affected by the violence, striving to mitigate the humanitarian crisis that ensues in such turbulent times.

The European Union has also stepped into the fray, advocating for a balanced approach that recognises Israel's right to defend itself while urging restraint to prevent further civilian casualties. The EU's diplomatic efforts often involve facilitating dialogue between conflicting parties, promoting peaceful negotiations, and funding humanitarian relief projects. This dual approach aims to stabilise the region, as repeated cycles of violence can exacerbate existing tensions, making long-term peace more elusive. The EU's involvement underscores the importance of multilateral action in addressing complex international conflicts.

Non-governmental organisations play a vital role in providing immediate humanitarian assistance and advocating for the rights of affected populations. Following the attack and the subsequent Israeli bombings, NGOs have mobilised to deliver food, medical supplies, and psychological support to those in need. Their grassroots efforts often complement the work of international organisations by addressing local needs and fostering community resilience. Additionally, these organisations frequently document human rights abuses, contributing to a broader understanding of the impact of violence on civilians and pressuring governments and international bodies to take action.

The interplay between international organisations and local entities is essential for sustainable peacebuilding. While international organisations provide the framework for diplomatic engagement and humanitarian support, local organisations often possess the cultural understanding and community connections necessary to implement effective solutions. In the context of the ongoing conflict in Israel and Gaza, collaboration between these different actors can lead to more comprehensive strategies that not only address immediate needs but also lay the groundwork for lasting peace. The role of international organisations, therefore, is not merely reactive; it is deeply intertwined with the proactive efforts required to foster a more stable and just environment for all parties involved.

Reactions from key nations

IN THE AFTERMATH OF the October 7th attack by Hamas, key nations reacted with a mixture of condemnation, support, and calls for restraint. The attack, which resulted in significant loss of life and heightened tensions in the region, prompted immediate responses from world leaders and governments. Israel's military response, which included extensive bombing campaigns in Gaza, further escalated the situation, leading to a complex web of international diplomatic reactions.

The United States, a longstanding ally of Israel, swiftly reaffirmed its support for the Israeli government. Statements from the White House emphasized Israel's right to defend itself against terrorist threats. American officials expressed solidarity with the Israeli people, offering military aid and intelligence support. However, there were also calls from various political factions within the U.S. for Israel to consider the humanitarian implications of its military actions, highlighting the need for a balanced approach that addresses both security concerns and civilian casualties.

European nations exhibited a range of responses, reflecting their diverse political landscapes and historical ties to the region. Countries such as Germany and France expressed unequivocal support for Israel's right to defend itself but simultaneously urged restraint to minimise civilian suffering in Gaza. The European Union called for an immediate ceasefire, advocating for humanitarian access to those affected by the conflict. This dual approach aimed to support Israel's security while also acknowledging the humanitarian crisis unfolding in the region, which has drawn widespread international concern.

In the Middle East, reactions were heavily influenced by regional dynamics and alliances. Nations such as Iran and Turkey condemned Israel's military actions, framing them as aggression against the Palestinian people. They rallied support for Hamas and called for solidarity among Muslim nations. Meanwhile, countries like Egypt and Jordan, which share borders with Israel and have peace treaties in place, found themselves in a delicate position, advocating for de-escalation while managing their own domestic pressures to support Palestinians. The reactions from these nations highlighted the intricate balance between political allegiance and the humanitarian crises that often arise from such conflicts.

Public opinion in various countries also played a significant role in shaping governmental responses. Protests erupted in many cities around the world, calling for an end to the violence and expressing solidarity with Palestinian civilians. Grassroots movements emphasized the need for a peaceful resolution and criticized both Hamas's initial attack and Israel's subsequent military response. These public sentiments influenced diplomatic discussions and were reflected in the positions taken by some governments, illustrating how popular opinion can intersect with international politics in times of crisis.

Public opinion worldwide regarding the aftermath of the October 7th attack by Hamas has been shaped by a complex interplay of historical context, media portrayal, and geopolitical interests. In the immediate aftermath of the attack, reactions varied significantly across different regions, influenced by existing narratives about the Israeli-Palestinian conflict. In many Western nations, there was strong initial support for Israel's right to defend itself against terrorism, reflecting a long-standing alignment with Israel's security concerns. However, this perspective was often counterbalanced by concerns over the humanitarian impact of military actions on Palestinian civilians, leading to a nuanced debate within public discourse.

In contrast, sentiments in Arab and Muslim-majority countries tended to be more sympathetic towards the Palestinian cause. Public opinion polls in these regions indicated widespread condemnation of the Israeli response, with many viewing the attack as a continuation of a long history of oppression. Social media played a crucial role in shaping these opinions, as images and narratives circulated rapidly, mobilising grassroots support and protests against perceived injustices. The emotional resonance of the conflict, particularly among younger generations, has led to increased activism and calls for solidarity with Palestinians.

In Europe, public opinion has been more divided, reflecting the continent's complex relationship with both Israel and Palestine. While some European governments expressed support for Israel's right to defend itself, there were significant public demonstrations advocating for Palestinian rights and an end to military operations in Gaza. This duality in public sentiment has prompted debates about the effectiveness of European foreign policy in the region and the need for a more balanced approach. The rise of anti-Semitic incidents in the wake of the conflict has also raised concerns about the broader implications of public discourse surrounding the issue.

The role of traditional media and social media platforms cannot be understated in shaping public perceptions. Mainstream media coverage often frames the narrative around national security and terrorism, which can overshadow the humanitarian aspects of the conflict. Conversely, social media allows for a more grassroots perspective, where individuals share personal stories and experiences that highlight the human cost of military actions. This divergence has led to polarised views, with some audiences gravitating towards more extreme positions based on the narratives they consume.

As the situation continues to evolve, public opinion worldwide remains fluid, subject to change as new developments unfold. The ongoing nature of the conflict, coupled with shifting alliances and international diplomacy efforts, will likely influence how societies perceive both the immediate and long-term consequences of the October 7th attack and Israel's subsequent military actions. Understanding these dynamics is essential for comprehending the broader implications for peace in the region and the international community's response to ongoing humanitarian crises.

Chapter 23: Media coverage and narrative

Media representations of the conflict following the October 7th attack by Hamas have played a crucial role in shaping public perception and understanding of the events that unfolded. Various news outlets, social media platforms, and international broadcasts have reported on the aftermath of the attack, often focusing on the immediate humanitarian crisis and the military response from Israel. The portrayal of these events varies significantly across different media channels, reflecting the diverse political, cultural, and social contexts in which they operate.

One prominent aspect of media representation involves the framing of the violence and its victims. Many outlets have highlighted the human cost of the conflict, emphasising civilian casualties and the destruction of infrastructure in Gaza. This focus fosters empathy and raises awareness of the humanitarian needs in the region. However, the narratives often differ, with some media emphasising the threat posed by Hamas, portraying the group as a terrorist organisation responsible for initiating the cycle of violence. This dichotomy in representation can lead to polarised opinions, where audiences either sympathise with the plight of the Palestinian people or view Israel's military actions as justified self-defence.

Social media has further complicated the narrative surrounding the conflict. Platforms like Twitter and Facebook have become battlegrounds for competing narratives, with users sharing personal stories, videos, and images that often go viral. Citizen journalism has emerged as a significant force, allowing individuals from both sides to present their perspectives. However, the rapid spread of misinformation and manipulated content can distort the reality of the situation, leading to confusion and further entrenching biases. This phenomenon underscores the need for critical media literacy among the public, enabling individuals to discern credible sources from those that perpetuate falsehoods.

International media coverage has also been influenced by geopolitical considerations. Different countries have varying interests in the conflict, which can lead to biased reporting. For example, Western media may focus on Israel's right to defend itself, while outlets in the Middle East might emphasize Palestinian suffering and resistance. These divergent narratives can affect international public opinion and diplomatic relations, as governments respond to the sentiments expressed by their citizens. The selective reporting of facts can yield a skewed understanding of the conflict's complexities, making it imperative for audiences to seek diverse viewpoints.

The repercussions of these media representations extend beyond immediate public opinion; they can influence policy decisions and humanitarian efforts. When media coverage emphasises the need for aid and support for affected populations, it can mobilise public and governmental action. Conversely, narratives that frame the conflict predominantly as a security issue may lead to policies that prioritise military responses over diplomatic solutions. Ultimately, the way media represents the aftermath of the October 7th attack will shape the long-term prospects for peace and stability in the region, making it a critical area of analysis for all stakeholders involved.

Social media has emerged as a powerful platform for shaping public perceptions, particularly in the context of geopolitical conflicts. Following the October 7th attack by Hamas, social media channels became inundated with images, videos, and narratives that significantly influenced how people viewed the events unfolding in Israel and Gaza. The rapid dissemination of information, often without verification, created an environment where emotions frequently overshadowed facts. This phenomenon demonstrates the unique capacity of social media to mold perceptions in real-time, often leading to polarised views that can exacerbate tensions rather than foster understanding.

The immediate aftermath of the October 7th attack saw a surge of content shared across various platforms, each piece contributing to a broader narrative about the conflict. Proponents of both sides utilised social media to present their perspectives, often framing their arguments in emotionally charged terms. This strategic use of social media enabled different factions to rally support, mobilize resources, and influence international opinions, underscoring the platform's significance in contemporary conflict dynamics. The speed at which information travelled meant that narratives were formed almost instantaneously, leaving little room for critical analysis or reflection among viewers.

Moreover, social media's algorithms often prioritize engagement over accuracy, further complicating the landscape of information. Content that elicits strong emotional reactions tends to be shared more widely, leading to the proliferation of sensationalised or misleading narratives. In the case of the October 7th attack and the subsequent Israeli bombings, many users encountered a barrage of images and messages that either vilified or glorified actions taken by both sides. This environment can create echo chambers, where individuals are only exposed to viewpoints that reinforce their existing beliefs, thereby hindering constructive dialogue and understanding.

The global reach of social media also means that perceptions shaped by these platforms can have far-reaching implications. International audiences, influenced by the narratives presented online, may form opinions that impact diplomatic relations and humanitarian responses. The portrayal of Israel's military actions in the wake of the attacks, for instance, faced scrutiny and condemnation from various global actors, often driven by the narratives circulating on social media. This interconnectedness highlights the responsibility that comes with sharing information and the potential consequences of perpetuating divisive narratives.

In conclusion, social media's role in shaping perceptions during and after the October 7th attack cannot be understated. While it serves as a tool for raising awareness and fostering solidarity, it also poses challenges in terms of misinformation and polarisation. As individuals navigate this complex landscape, it is essential to approach the content critically, recognising the power of social media not only to inform but also to distort public understanding of critical issues. Ultimately, fostering informed discussions and promoting media literacy will be vital in mitigating the adverse effects of social media on public perceptions surrounding the ongoing conflict.

The impact of propaganda

THE IMPACT OF PROPAGANDA in the aftermath of the October 7th attack by Hamas is multifaceted, shaping public perceptions and influencing the responses of both the Israeli government and the global community. In the immediate wake of the attack, narratives emerged that sought to frame the event in a context that suited various political agendas. Propaganda played a critical role in mobilising support, justifying military responses, and solidifying national identity within Israel. The portrayal of the attack as a direct threat not only galvanised public opinion but also created an environment where dissenting voices were often overshadowed by a dominant narrative of victimisation and urgency.

Media outlets, both local and international, became battlegrounds for competing narratives. Israeli media tended to emphasise the brutality of the attack and the necessity of a robust military response, framing the actions as defensive measures against terrorism. This portrayal resonated with many in the public, fostering a sense of unity and national resolve. Conversely, some international media highlighted the humanitarian crisis resulting from the subsequent bombings in Gaza, portraying the situation as a tragic cycle of violence. The interplay between these narratives illustrates how propaganda can manipulate the framing of events to evoke specific emotional responses and shape public discourse.

Social media also emerged as a powerful tool for propaganda, with both sides utilising platforms to disseminate information rapidly. In Israel, social media campaigns aimed to bolster morale, share survivor stories, and encourage support for military actions. These narratives often emphasised themes of resilience and national pride. Meanwhile, groups sympathetic to the Palestinian cause utilised social media to highlight civilian casualties and humanitarian needs in Gaza, framing the Israeli military response as excessive and indiscriminate. The viral nature of social media ensured that these messages reached global audiences, further complicating the discourse surrounding the conflict.

The impact of propaganda extends beyond immediate public opinion; it also influences policy decisions and international relations. Governments and organisations monitor these narratives to gauge public sentiment and adjust their diplomatic strategies accordingly. The Israeli government's ongoing military operations were, in part, justified through the lens of propaganda that depicted Hamas as a persistent threat. Conversely, international calls for restraint and humanitarian considerations were often framed as attempts to curtail Israel's right to defend itself, complicating diplomatic efforts and creating rifts among allies.

Ultimately, the pervasive influence of propaganda in the aftermath of the October 7th attack underscores the importance of critical media literacy among the public. As narratives evolve, individuals must navigate a landscape filled with biased information and emotionally charged rhetoric. Understanding the mechanisms of propaganda can empower citizens to discern fact from fiction, fostering a more nuanced dialogue about the conflict and its broader implications. The ability to critically evaluate information is essential for promoting peace and reconciliation in a region deeply scarred by violence and misunderstanding.

Chapter 24: Long-term consequences

Political ramifications for Israel and Palestine

The October 7th attack by Hamas marked a significant turning point in the enduring conflict between Israel and Palestine, leading to a complex web of political ramifications for both parties involved. The immediate response from Israel was a military escalation, characterised by extensive bombing campaigns aimed at Hamas infrastructure in Gaza. This reaction was not only a show of military strength but also served to solidify domestic support for the Israeli government amidst a climate of fear and uncertainty. The political landscape shifted dramatically as citizens rallied behind their leaders, reinforcing the notion that strong military action was essential for national security.

On the Palestinian side, the aftermath of the attack and subsequent Israeli bombings had a profound impact on the political dynamics within Gaza and the West Bank. The escalation heightened tensions between Hamas and the Palestinian Authority, which governs the West Bank. As Hamas positioned itself as the defender of Palestinian rights in the wake of the bombings, the authority of the Palestinian leadership was called into question. Many Palestinians, feeling abandoned by their leaders, began to look towards Hamas for guidance and support, potentially eroding the Palestinian Authority's grip on power and complicating future governance and peace negotiations.

Internationally, the bombing campaign drew widespread criticism and calls for restraint from various governments and organisations around the world. The humanitarian crisis resulting from the bombings escalated tensions, prompting protests and diplomatic efforts aimed at mediating a ceasefire. Countries that traditionally supported Israel found themselves under pressure to advocate for humanitarian aid and protection of civilians in Gaza. This created a nuanced dynamic in international relations, as allies of Israel grappled with balancing their support for its right to defend itself with the growing humanitarian concerns raised by the global community.

The political ramifications extended to Israel's relationships with its Arab neighbours and the broader Muslim world. The perception of Israeli military actions as disproportionate fuelled anti-Israel sentiment across the region, leading to renewed calls for solidarity with the Palestinian cause. This shift could jeopardise normalisation agreements that had been established between Israel and several Arab states, as public opinion in those nations increasingly leaned towards supporting Palestinian rights. The potential fracturing of these diplomatic ties could have long-lasting consequences for regional stability and security.

In conclusion, the political ramifications of the October 7th attack and the ensuing Israeli military response are far-reaching and multifaceted. The immediate effects on domestic politics within both Israel and Palestine set the stage for a potentially volatile environment, where leadership legitimacy and public support are continuously challenged. The international community's reaction further complicates the situation, as humanitarian concerns intersect with geopolitical interests. As the aftermath continues to unfold, the need for a sustainable resolution to the conflict remains more pressing than ever, underscoring the intricate connections between military actions and political outcomes in this deeply divided region.

The psychological impact on civilians following the October 7th attack and the subsequent Israeli bombing is profound and multifaceted. In the wake of such violence, individuals experience a range of psychological responses, including trauma, anxiety, and depression. The direct exposure to conflict can result in post-traumatic stress disorder (PTSD) for many, as the memories of the attack and the sounds of bombings linger long after the immediate danger has passed. This trauma does not only affect those who were directly involved in the violence but also extends to families and communities, creating a ripple effect that complicates recovery and healing.

Children, in particular, are highly susceptible to the psychological fallout from conflict. Many young individuals are exposed to distressing events, leading to developmental issues and lasting emotional scars. Symptoms such as nightmares, heightened anxiety, and behavioural problems can emerge, affecting their ability to engage in regular childhood activities and education.

These experiences can hinder their long-term mental health and well-being, leading to a cycle of distress that can persist into adulthood. The loss of a safe environment disrupts their sense of security, which is crucial for healthy development.

The impact on adults is equally significant. Many individuals face the challenge of coping with the loss of loved ones, homes, and livelihoods. Grief and loss can manifest as depression, leading to a sense of hopelessness that permeates daily life. The stress of rebuilding after destruction, coupled with the constant threat of further violence, can exacerbate feelings of isolation and despair. Economic instability and the inability to provide for one's family further complicate the psychological landscape, creating a sense of helplessness among those affected by the conflict.

Moreover, community cohesion can suffer as trust erodes in the aftermath of violence. Civilians may become suspicious of one another, leading to social fragmentation that hampers collective recovery efforts. Support systems that once existed may weaken, as individuals focus on their own survival. This breakdown of community ties can exacerbate mental health issues, as social support is a critical component of resilience. The psychological toll of mistrust and disconnection can hinder the rebuilding process, making it difficult for communities to heal together.

In addressing the psychological needs of civilians, it is essential to implement comprehensive mental health support systems. This includes access to counselling services, community programs aimed at fostering social connections, and initiatives to promote resilience. Governments and organisations must prioritise mental health as a critical aspect of recovery, recognising that the psychological scars of conflict can linger for generations. By addressing these needs, society can begin to heal and move toward a more stable and peaceful future, acknowledging that the price of peace extends beyond the cessation of violence to include the mental well-being of its citizens.

Future of peace efforts

THE FUTURE OF PEACE efforts in the wake of the October 7th attack by Hamas hinges on a complex interplay of military, diplomatic, and societal factors. Following the attack, Israel's military response has been intense and widespread, aiming to neutralise perceived threats and restore security. However, such military actions risk perpetuating a cycle of violence that undermines long-term peace prospects. Understanding the dynamics of this conflict is crucial for stakeholders looking to foster an environment conducive to negotiation and reconciliation.

International actors play a pivotal role in shaping the future of peace in the region. The responses from countries around the world, particularly those in the Middle East, will significantly influence the trajectory of peace efforts. Diplomatic initiatives, including ceasefire agreements or peace talks, must be supported by a robust framework that includes humanitarian aid and reconstruction efforts. The involvement of global powers can facilitate dialogue, but it must be balanced with respect for the sovereignty of local populations and their legitimate aspirations for peace and security.

Grassroots movements and civil society organisations are essential in promoting peace from the ground up. These entities often have a deep understanding of local grievances and can bridge divides between communities. Their efforts in fostering dialogue and mutual understanding can complement top-down approaches, creating a more holistic peace process. Promoting reconciliation at the community level may help to address the deep-seated animosities that fuel ongoing violence, thereby laying the groundwork for a more sustainable peace.

Technological advancements can also shape the future of peace efforts. Innovations in communication and information dissemination can facilitate awareness and advocacy for peace initiatives. Social media platforms, for example, can amplify voices calling for peace and create networks of solidarity among diverse groups. However, they can also spread misinformation and incite further violence, underscoring the need for responsible use of technology in peacebuilding efforts. Harnessing these tools effectively will require a concerted effort from both local and international actors.

Ultimately, the future of peace efforts in the aftermath of the October 7th attack depends on a collective commitment to addressing the underlying issues that fuel conflict. This includes a revaluation of narratives around security and justice, as well as a willingness to engage in difficult conversations about rights, recognition, and coexistence. As various stakeholders navigate this complex landscape, the potential for meaningful progress hinges on their ability to prioritize dialogue over destruction, fostering a future where peace can prevail.

Chapter 25: Lessons learned and moving forward

Analysing historical patterns

Analysing historical patterns is crucial in understanding the aftermath of the October 7th attack by Hamas and the subsequent Israeli bombing campaign. Historical context sheds light on the recurring cycles of violence, responses, and peace efforts that have defined the Israeli-Palestinian conflict. By examining past conflicts and their resolutions, we can gain insights into the motivations behind actions taken by both sides and the long-term implications that follow.

One significant pattern observed in the history of conflicts in this region is the cycle of retaliation. Following an attack, Israel has frequently resorted to military action as a means of deterrence and to reassert its security. The October 7th attack marked a particularly intense escalation, and the Israeli response was in line with its historical approach of conducting airstrikes targeting Hamas infrastructure. This pattern illustrates how immediate threats often provoke swift and substantial military responses, which can perpetuate a cycle of violence rather than facilitating dialogue or peace.

Moreover, the historical context of previous ceasefires and peace negotiations reveals a consistent difficulty in achieving lasting resolutions. Efforts such as the Oslo Accords or the Camp David Summit show that while there have been moments of potential reconciliation, underlying grievances and mistrust have often undermined progress. This pattern highlights the complex interplay of political, social, and economic factors that contribute to ongoing hostilities and the challenge of moving beyond immediate military responses to address root causes.

The international community's role in these historical patterns cannot be overlooked. Various nations and organisations have attempted to mediate peace, often influenced by their political interests and alliances. The aftermath of the October 7th attack saw renewed calls for intervention and support for both humanitarian aid and a possible ceasefire. However, the effectiveness of these interventions has varied, and historical patterns suggest that without addressing the fundamental issues of sovereignty, security, and mutual recognition, such efforts may fall short of creating sustainable peace.

In conclusion, analysing historical patterns following the October 7th attack provides essential insights into the dynamics of the Israeli-Palestinian conflict. By understanding the cyclical nature of violence and the challenges of negotiation, we can better comprehend the complexities involved in fostering peace. The lessons drawn from past conflicts serve as a reminder that while military responses may offer immediate security, they often fail to address the deeper issues at play, emphasizing the urgent need for innovative approaches to conflict resolution and dialogue.

Strategies for conflict resolution

EFFECTIVE CONFLICT resolution strategies are essential in addressing the aftermath of the October 7th attack by Hamas and the subsequent Israeli bombing. The complexities of the situation necessitate a multifaceted approach that considers the historical context, emotional grievances, and the broader geopolitical landscape. One crucial strategy involves fostering dialogue between conflicting parties. Open communication allows for the expression of grievances and the exploration of underlying issues. Initiatives that encourage face-to-face conversations can help humanize adversaries, create empathy, and pave the way for understanding.

Mediation serves as another vital tool in conflict resolution. Neutral third parties can facilitate discussions, helping to bridge gaps between conflicting sides. In the context of the Israeli-Palestinian conflict, international mediators can provide a platform for negotiations that might otherwise be impossible. These mediators can assist in establishing ground rules, managing emotional responses, and ensuring that all voices are heard. The involvement of respected figures or organizations can lend credibility to the mediation process and encourage more constructive dialogue.

Another effective strategy is the implementation of confidence-building measures. These actions can gradually reduce tensions and foster trust between conflicting parties. For example, initiatives aimed at improving humanitarian conditions in affected areas can demonstrate goodwill and a commitment to peace. Additionally, joint projects that bring together individuals from both sides can help shift perceptions, creating a sense of shared interest and mutual benefit. Confidence-building measures can serve as stepping stones toward more meaningful negotiations by establishing a foundation of trust.

Education and awareness-raising campaigns also play a critical role in conflict resolution. By promoting understanding of the historical narratives and perspectives of both Israelis and Palestinians, these campaigns can help dispel myths and reduce bias. Educational programs can foster a culture of peace by teaching conflict resolution skills and encouraging critical thinking. In the aftermath of violent events, it is crucial to counteract narratives of hatred and division with messages of coexistence and mutual respect.

Finally, long-term solutions require addressing the root causes of the conflict. This involves recognizing and tackling systemic issues such as inequality, lack of access to resources, and political disenfranchisement. Comprehensive peace agreements should include provisions for social justice, economic development, and political representation for all affected communities. By addressing these underlying factors, stakeholders can work towards sustainable peace that not only resolves immediate tensions but also lays the groundwork for a more stable and harmonious future.

Building a sustainable peace framework

BUILDING A SUSTAINABLE peace framework in the aftermath of the October 7th attack requires a multi-faceted approach that addresses the underlying issues contributing to the cycle of violence. The immediate response to the attack, including military actions such as bombings, may provide a short-term sense of security but often fails to lay the groundwork for lasting peace. A sustainable peace framework must prioritise dialogue, reconciliation, and understanding among all parties involved, acknowledging that military solutions alone are insufficient to resolve deep-rooted conflicts.

One essential element of this framework is the inclusion of diverse voices in the peace process. Engaging various stakeholders, including community leaders, civil society organizations, and representatives from both Israeli and Palestinian populations, can help ensure that the resulting agreements reflect a broader consensus. This inclusive approach fosters a sense of ownership and commitment to the peace process among all parties, reducing the likelihood of future escalations. Additionally, involving women and youth in discussions can introduce new perspectives and innovative solutions that traditional leaders may overlook.

Another critical aspect is addressing the humanitarian needs of affected populations. The aftermath of the October 7th attack has exacerbated existing social and economic disparities, leading to increased suffering among civilians. A sustainable peace framework must prioritize humanitarian aid, economic development, and infrastructure rebuilding in both Israel and the Palestinian territories. By improving living conditions and providing opportunities for growth, the framework can help reduce resentment and foster a more cooperative environment conducive to peace.

Education plays a pivotal role in building a sustainable peace framework. Initiatives aimed at promoting mutual understanding and respect between Israeli and Palestinian communities can help break down stereotypes and build trust. Educational programs that emphasize shared values, history, and the importance of coexistence can create a new generation of leaders committed to peaceful resolution rather than violence. Investing in educational exchanges and collaborative projects can further enhance dialogue and break the cycle of mistrust that has long plagued the region.

Finally, international support and oversight are vital for the success of any sustainable peace framework. The involvement of neutral third parties can provide essential mediation and facilitate ongoing dialogue. Moreover, international actors can help ensure compliance with peace agreements and hold parties accountable for violations. By fostering an environment of cooperation and support, the international community can play a crucial role in reinforcing the principles of a sustainable peace framework, ultimately contributing to a more stable and secure future for both Israelis and Palestinians.

Recommended reading & references:

1. The Sykes-Picot Agreement of 1916 was a pivotal moment in the history of Arab nationalism. In this secret arrangement, Britain and France divided the Middle Eastern territories of the collapsing Ottoman Empire into spheres of influence, with little regard for the ethnic and religious complexities of the region.
2. The Sykes-Picot Agreement of 1916 epitomised the European powers' disregard for Arab aspirations and national identities. This secret arrangement between Britain and France, with Russian assent, outlined the division of Ottoman territories into spheres of influence, effectively disregarding the existing cultural and historical ties within the region.
3. United Nations resolutions, such as Resolution 242, call for the withdrawal of Israeli forces from occupied territories
4. The establishment of the State of Israel in 1948 marked a pivotal moment in Palestinian history, resulting in the Nakba, or "catastrophe," where an estimated 700,000 Palestinians were forcibly displaced from their homes
5. The 1917 Balfour Declaration marked a significant turning point, as it expressed British support for the establishment of a "national home for the Jewish people" in Palestine, without consulting the indigenous Arab population.
6. The 1967 Six-Day War further exacerbated the situation, as Israel occupied the West Bank and Gaza Strip, along with other territories. This occupation introduced a regime of military rule characterised by land expropriation and settlement expansion.
7. The Fourth Geneva Convention prohibits the transfer of an occupying power's civilian population into occupied territory and

restricts the appropriation of land for military purposes.
8. Hague Convention for the Protection of Cultural Property in the Event of Armed Conflict emphasise the responsibility of states to safeguard cultural sites during times of conflict
9. Jewish prisoners of war in Gilgil Kenya
10. The Gilgil camp was officially opened in 1941, initially designed to house Italian prisoners captured during the East African Campaign. However, as the war progressed and geopolitical dynamics shifted, the camp began to accommodate Jewish soldiers, many of whom were captured in North Africa or were refugees from Europe who had joined the Allied forces. The camp's population grew significantly, leading to the implementation of various protocols to manage the diverse group of detainees, which included not only Jews but also other nationalities and backgrounds.
11. The objectives of Hamas are rooted in its ideological framework, which centres on resistance against Israeli occupation and the pursuit of Palestinian self-determination. Hamas positions itself not only as a political entity but also as a social movement, providing essential services such as education, healthcare, and welfare to many Gazans.

Also by DM Ole Kiminta

How the Western Democracies failed the world
Supporting Refugees in their Homelands
Dissuading Global War Mongers:
Dissuading war mongers
La Libération Monétaire en Afrique
Canada Post: Management failure to modernise mail systems
Canada Post management failure to modernise mail systems
Canada Post: Management failure to modernise mail systems
Live to be 200
Aim to live for 200
Aim to live to be 200
Western democracies failed the world economies
Wrong foot forward: US-Canada trade wars
Canada begs to differ: Never a 51st state of USA
Tethered to the Kitchen
Nous ne pouvons pas être le 51e État des États-Unis
Nous ne serons jamais le 51ème état des États-Unis.
The Nephilim and the erosion of moral boundaries
Every human is an advocate for World Peace
The diplomatic dilemma of Western Sahara
Every human: Advocate for World Peace
The last blue planet
Europeans divided & shaped Arab World

www.ingramcontent.com/pod-product-compliance
Lightning Source LLC
Chambersburg PA
CBHW032125090426
42743CB00007B/464